AF227899

Lifetime Love 2-in-1 Connection Collection

Finding Your Soulmate + Long Distance Love - The #1 Lovers Collection for finding love and making love work long distance.

By Christopher Conway

© COPYRIGHT 2021 - ALL RIGHTS RESERVED.

The content contained within this book may not be reproduced, duplicated, or transmitted without direct written permission from the author or the publisher.

Under no circumstances will any blame or legal responsibility be held against the publisher, or author, for any damages, reparation, or monetary loss due to the information contained within this book. Either directly or indirectly.

Legal Notice:

This book is copyright protected. This book is only for personal use. You cannot amend, distribute, sell, use, quote, or paraphrase any part, or the content within this book, without the author or publisher's consent.

Disclaimer Notice:

Please note the information contained within this document is for educational and entertainment purposes only. All effort has been executed to present accurate, up-to-date, and reliable, complete information. No warranties of any kind are declared or implied. Readers acknowledge that the author is not engaging in the rendering of legal, financial, medical, or professional advice. The content within this book has been derived from various sources. Please consult a licensed professional before attempting any techniques outlined in this book.

By reading this document, the reader agrees that under no circumstances is the author responsible for any losses, direct or indirect, which are incurred as a result of the use of the information contained within this document, including, but not limited to, — errors, omissions, or inaccuracies.

YOUR FREE GIFT

Finding Your Soulmate Tips Sheet

Sometimes you need a quick tip for a situation. This tips sheet points you to the best resources to help you fast!

(Get Yours Now...It's FREE)

Request FREE Tips Sheet Today. Go to:
https://loveblueprints.com/soulmate-tips-sheet/

2-IN-1 BUNDLE TABLE OF CONTENTS

INTRODUCTION

Being lonely is not a pleasant experience. Trust me; **I know how you feel, so let me help you experience happiness**.

Oh, lest I forget, it is the happiness that comes from having someone special to hug, kiss, and do kinky things with.

You wake up each night, rollover, and wonder if the love of your life will ever be sleeping next to you. Is it your destiny to find your soulmate, or are you cursed to only date mediocrity?

Bad feelings over past relationships might linger, causing you to feel emotional depression occasionally. Even with the avalanche of relationship advice out there, it may still feel like nothing works for you.

What if today you have the solution in your hands? The question remains- will you use it?

There truly is a blueprint to finding your soulmate. It's not posted online for free; otherwise, everyone would have it and utilize it. This blueprint is in your hands if you will only open it and follow the actionable steps.

Say goodbye to finding a date on your own or asking friends and family to set you up with someone. The entire process should start with you. It's not complex; nor is it beyond your abilities.

What you need to do and how you should approach this self-preparation process for finding your divine love are exclusively and explicitly detailed in this blueprint you now have in your hands.

The journey to finding your soulmate starts with preparing your mind and soul to accept love. You must also know the types of people you should avoid, followed by a series of steps to find your soulmate *(or have this person find you)*.

Sprinkle in knowledge to identify signs that you have met your divine love and your life sails towards everlasting love. You will also learn the secret of sustaining a newfound love interest and how to maintain a balance between physical and spiritual connection.

True, there are several books available claiming to help with finding a soulmate.

The problem with most of these books is that they

are just details of someone's love story. The story may be interesting, the plot captivating, but you are left wanting actionable steps towards finding divine love.

Those personal love stories are nothing more than a touch of erotica wrapped with spirituality. They're one person's story of how they found their soulmate, and maybe you can do the same, IF you are just like them, but you are unique. They tell you to *'manifest'* your soulmate, and *'poof,'* they will appear.

I can assure you that your life and view of relationships might be vastly different than those authors. If you're an action-taker with achievements under your belt, you already know that thinking and believing never makes a miracle come true.

Merely doing what those authors did may not yield the results that you want. You already know that to get what you want out of life; you must take the proper steps and avoid pitfalls.

What you need is the proper mindset and steps used by thousands who found their soulmates. That is what I give you in this program, and that is why you will love this one.

I have compiled the actionable steps and mindset shifts used by couples who found their divine love. Use this blueprint, follow the steps, and find your soulmate quickly.

Why You Need to Use This Program

Just imagine your life full of the happiness you've been dreaming about since you were a teenager. Imagine a life where you experience daily love from someone that shares your belief system.

This person can almost finish your sentences. They feel pain when you feel it and look for ways to make that pain go away. And you happily do the same for them— no more mental or physical loneliness.

You wake up daily to their smile, and right away, you know your day will be nothing but joyful. You hurry to complete your daily tasks at work because you can't wait to get home and see your soulmate again. Isn't that what you've been dreaming about night after night?

As you digest this program, take time to ponder, not daydream, about following the simple steps highlighted and how you can put them into practice. If you've been doing something the wrong way before now, *'empty your cup,'* so to speak, start doing things the correct way. You will benefit from it if you understand the points therein instead of rushing through everything.

Here is something else you can do: after each *chapter (carefully written to solve one problem at a time)* -- work at implementing the lessons from that chapter before moving on to the next. Then you can track your progress and be sure that you've benefitted from this program.

As you go through this program, you will realize that true love involves several little things that might be important to the other person, which you may not count as significant.

You will also learn how to transition from the 'honeymoon' phase of a new relationship to the *making it work* phase, where conflicting views and disagreements may threaten your peace of mind.

You will also get to learn about love languages and why they are essential in a healthy relationship.

Here are positive reviews from readers:

"After reading just the first 12 pages of 'Finding Your Soulmate,' I knew this program would be a winner. No woo-woo fluff like most books. Just pure actionable steps to finding your soulmate."

Edgar Stark – Cape May, NJ

"Thanks for your advanced copy. Finally, a blueprint that shows you the steps to finding true love, not some think, and he/she will find you nonsense."

Bethanie Silverman – McCall, ID

As you have seen, my concern is not just publishing 'any' kind of love program but giving people what can add real value to your quest for true love.

My Promise to You About Finding Your Soulmate

What do you stand to benefit from after reading this fascinating *'soulmate blueprint'*? When you complete this blueprint, you will have the mindset and actionable steps to go into the world to find your soulmate or have your soulmate find you.

Not only will you have the skillset to find your love, but you will also have techniques to position yourself to be discovered by your divine love. You will gain confidence and readiness to find love, and you will have mastered the art of sustaining a relationship even when confronted with the *'unexpected.'*

You will have reduced emotional stress while enjoying your night's rest, and depression out of loneliness will be alleviated. You will also be poised to help others find their soulmate.

You see, it is like getting two products for the price of one- you will help yourself and those who are willing to listen to you.

Why You Cannot Wait Any Longer to Use this Blueprint

To be blunt- you are not getting any younger. The clock is ticking, and each day that goes by, you lose an opportunity to meet your soulmate. Scare tactics? Well, yes, because it is true. Don't be so gullible in believing that love will come to you when you are not looking for it.

Motivational speakers can make you lose that sense of urgency, claiming that *'love is what happens when you are busy with other things.'* While it is not impossible, it rarely happens.

Take, for instance, someone who wants a job. Will this person wait for a job, or will they look for it? You'll agree that they need to look for a job if they don't want to remain unemployed. So waiting for love to happen is not a good strategy.

It's now time to re-orientate your mindset about love. Finding your soulmate is more than mere fantasy. You must set out to 'find' love. Instead of believing that love 'just' happens, why not start accepting the reality? The reality is that attraction can happen at any time. Understand that attraction is not the same as love.

You Need to Act Before that Attraction Can Lead to a Conversation

You also need to **act** before that conversation can lead to a regular conversation. And before an ordinary conversation can lead to an emotional attachment, you also need to **take more action.** You do not want to appear desperate because someone might quickly feel they can take advantage of you.

As long as you believe the widespread fallacy that love happens, the possibility of finding your soulmate is reduced daily. Be determined to change that mindset today and make that decision without delay. I don't want you to remain single against your will longer than you planned to. I am sure you don't want that either.

Work on your mood, be happy and be propelled by positive vibes. Happy people attract happy people. If you don't work on yourself, your chances of finding a soulmate might get cut in half.

If you occasionally struggle with depression, think carefully about the cause and what you can do to minimize such feelings. If you need to enlist the aid of a therapist, please do so.

Change your mindset if you have always believed in sexual gratification over platonic relationships. Remember that a good friend makes a better lover.

So be interested in building genuine friendships and not just looking for sexual attraction. Learn to differentiate between attraction, lust, and true love.

What You Should Know About This Blueprint

I know that you are ready to learn the 'how', the 'what,' and the 'when' for finding love. While I am so anxious to share all those with you, too, there is something you must understand about finding your soulmate.

This blueprint also explains how a relationship's golden rule works. The golden law for relationship states: *"do unto your partner what they want done to them."* That contrasts with the known golden rule to treat others the way you want to be treated.

In relationships, treating your partner how you want to be treated can cause severe damage because how they want to be treated may be different from your idea of being a good person.

You will also learn how to make someone fall in love with you, not by coercing them but by silent persuasion. Each chapter starts with a small introduction to highlight crucial lessons embedded in the chapter.

This program cannot take into consideration every situation that you might find yourself facing. Apart from that, what is applicable in one country or region may not be acceptable in another part because cultural factors differ. So while I present general advice, it is left to you to personalize and apply each lesson.

How to Start the Process to Meeting Your Soulmate this Weekend

They say, *"what is worth doing is worth doing well."* The other part of that nugget is that what is worth doing is worth doing fast. Don't wait until summer or your next vacation before implementing the tips in this soulmate blueprint. This next weekend presents an opportunity for you to start finding your special someone.

The weekend is a great time to start because people are more likely to meet and relate more on weekends. Weekends also present an opportunity for a more relaxed atmosphere, away from weekday hustles and stress.

People generally unwind and feel calmer on weekends than during business days. So, learn the secrets of finding your soulmate and unleash your new ideas on the weekend.

It is time to transform your life. Start using the actionable steps in this blueprint this weekend to find your divine love *(or have them find you)*. Do a favor for a friend and tell them about this program or buy it for them. Do not keep this valuable information all to yourself. Remember, read to understand, and do not rush over each of the topics. It will be a journey, and I will be your tour guide!

See you on the inside!

CHAPTER 1: PREPARING YOUR MIND & SOUL TO ACCEPT LOVE

Just as you need to cultivate a piece of land before crops can grow on it, the mind and soul need to be well-prepared to accept love. In this chapter, you will learn how to get ready for finding your soulmate.

You will know why it is essential to let go of any lingering past negativity and understand what you want in a potential soulmate.

Impact of Negative Thoughts

Negative thoughts will only bring negativity. We can all cultivate love, and we are all loveable. But your past negative experiences will want you to believe that no matter how much you try again, the result will not be any different from how it turned out the last time.

The past affects how the mind thinks and how we emotionally react to certain situations. It can even worsen if your brain subconsciously tries to make up for one's failures in a past relationship. What if your past love has caused you great emotional harm, and you feel you must get back at them?

Here is what Dr. Rhodes, a psychologist, and a dating coach, said:

> *"Our childhood experiences with our parents and our teachers and our friends do have a pretty big impact on how we operate both personally and professionally in early adulthood."*

As you try to avoid bad past experiences and work around any insecurities, it may reduce your chance of finding love again. To successfully find your soulmate, you must first learn to let go of past relationships and any pain those relationships caused.

What Could Be Holding You Back From Love

How will you know if you are still holding on to negative energies from past relationships? Here are some warning signs:

Making comparisons

If your past relationship is the yardstick for finding a soulmate, that is a clear sign that you may still be holding on to lingering thoughts from your past.

You might feel a need to find someone new but may want every detail about this new person *(how they look, how they smile, how they express love)* to be patterned after a past relationship.

Realize that two people are not the same, and no two relationships will be the same. These kinds of comparisons will hold you back from finding love because if your search does not produce something more like your past relationship, you will find it difficult to express love with someone new.

Living in a fantasy world

While there is nothing wrong with fantasizing about what you desire, if you continuously fantasize about a past relationship, that is another sign that you may still be holding on to the past.

If you always dream about sharing a warm embrace with a past love, having dinner with them, or going on a vacation with them, slow down a little and pay attention to yourself. You are not ready for a relationship. Spend more time letting go before inviting someone new into your life.

Talking about your past relationship

What a person talks about reflects what is in their heart. Do this now: think about how often you talk about your ex or your past relationships.

What is your answer? Often? More often than necessary? Or rarely? How you respond to this question determines if you are mentally ready for a new relationship or not.

If *'often'* and *'more often than necessary'* are one of your answers, it is a warning sign that you may still be holding on to the past. If you are holding onto past relationships, you will try to twist conversations with someone new towards your ex.

Doing this will only chase a new person away. This person will start to show less interest in you because people know when your focus is not on them but instead on someone else.

Keeping pace with your ex

You may claim to be over a past romance, but your actions show something different. You constantly research your ex online, maybe on social media or any other means available.

You feel as if it is your right to know everything about your ex, the same way you did when you two were together.

While this 'spying' may seem fun and worthwhile when you are bored, it is another warning sign that you are still holding on to a past relationship.

You may get hurt investigating your ex, only to discover that this person has moved forward with their world and not thinking about you anymore.

Wanting to get back at your ex

If you still feel like getting back at your ex, either for an affair or over another thing, that is a bad sign. It is an indication that you are still not over your former relationship.

You will bring that angry energy around new people that you meet. People can feel your anger, and when someone feels your anger, they become less interested in you.

Sure, they might not tell you. At first, someone new seemed interested, but their interest will fade after a few minutes, and you will not be sure why. The anger inside you will always chase away new love.

Brewing over hurt feelings

Okay, so you've had a negative experience with an ex. Perhaps it was emotional or physical abuse. Maybe it was the depressing effect of hurtful words, or maybe what hurt you was their infidelity.

If a considerable amount of time has passed since the incident and you are still fuming over what happened, it may be a cue that you are still not over that relationship.

This issue is different than just being angry. It's about pitying yourself. Oh, *"poor me,"* you say to yourself. *"I am sick of people doing bad things to me,"* you scream inside your head.

It would help if you stopped pitying yourself as the victim. A victim mentality does not attract love; it repels love.

Getting Over Negative Thoughts & Past Relationships

If you are still holding on to negativity from past relationships, understand that finding a soulmate will be a difficult thing to do. Now is when you want to prepare your mind for new love by getting over past negative feelings.

If you do not, this will negatively impact new relationships because you will be extra cautious about expressing your intentions and interests. Apart from that, you may criticize new people you meet because of unrealistic comparisons to your past.

Think about how they will feel knowing that someone from your past has a significant influence over how and what you do?

This outside influence will not help a new relationship grow! Instead of dealing with this type of situation, do not create this type of problem at all. Do whatever you can to move away from a negative past before starting any new relationship.

If you have thoughts about reconciling with your ex, realize that the chances are very slim. In the likelihood that you think you can repair your past relationship, understand that the problems you had before will resurface, whether you like it or not. Remember the cliché phrase, *"a leopard does not change its spots."*

Trust me; you do not want to return to a relationship that will give you neither joy nor love. Live in the present and not in your past thoughts. Believe that you are lovable even if your ex made you feel that you were not. Work on building your confidence.

If you want to build your confidence, speak with your friends, and ask them how they feel about you. It's reassuring to know that they appreciate you and enjoy spending time with you.

That way, you will know that **only** your ex felt differently about you. Next, do all you can to be as generous and hospitable to other people. Please don't do it because you want others to speak well of you, but because you want your actions to be the **new you.**

The point is that when you **know** that you can contribute real value to the lives of others, your confidence grows that you have value. Be happy with your life and with the decisions that you make.

Realize that splitting with your ex was the best possible decision you could have made at the time instead of brewing over being single. Avoid knowing too much or following what your ex Is doing in their life. The less you know about your ex's current life, the better for you.

While you may not need to delete your social media accounts, never search through social media because of curiosity about what your ex is doing. Get past the urge to track their life.

The less you know about your ex's current life, the easier it will be for you to start a new life without them.

Once you develop beyond your past relationship, then you can claim readiness to find your soulmate. Do you think these steps are doable? They are simple things you can do, but if they seem overwhelming, try this instead.

Take each task one step at a time instead of trying to implement everything at once. Believe that you can move past negative feelings and have an open heart to find your soulmate.

But that's not all you must do to get ready; you need to understand what you want in a new relationship.

A Proper View of Past Relationships

They say that every disappointment is a blessing in disguise. That is true of a failed romance because even though it hurts, there are many lessons to learn. Take a moment to ponder about your past relationships in order to itemize the following:

- What were the high points of the relationship?

- What memories will you want to keep?

These two questions will help you identify what you want to hold on to in your next relationship. Next, give careful thoughts to the following questions:

- When and how did the relationship turn sour?

- What mistakes did you make, and what should you have done differently?

- What did your ex do to hurt you?

Answers to these questions can help you to identify what you need to start doing differently in your new relationship. It will also help you know what can hurt you and what you need to change about yourself in order to not hurt your new partner.

The point is that you need to learn from failed past relationships instead of brewing over what occurred. Remember, what's happened has happened, and you can't turn back the hands of time.

However, you can use your past relationship as a stepping stone to achieving something more significant in the future.

As mentioned earlier, you need to get over a past relationship before moving forward to find your soulmate.

Have a Clear Vision of What You Want in Life

The next thing you must do to prepare your mind for a soulmate is to identify your goals.

- What do you want out of life?

- What type of person are you?

- What interests you, as well as irritates you?

Your answer to these questions reveals something interesting about you. These facts indicate what you want out of life and should influence your choice of a soulmate.

Maybe you used a past selection process that did not consider your answers to the questions above. Just choosing someone because they are attractive and have a cool or sexy 'style' usually ends with feeling as if you did not get value out of the relationship.

One day beauty fades, and someone's cool or sexy 'style' becomes irrelevant. That once physically attractive person may start developing wrinkled skin and a less beautiful body. When this happens, nothing else will matter except your desire for appreciation and companionship.

So, ask yourself again: *"what do you want from life?"* If you successfully identify what you want from life, it will not be hard for you to find someone who wants the same so that you reach your goals.

There are cases when the person you find attractive may not share your view of career, parenting, caring for in-laws, and health. They may even share a different idea of being successful. What about 'simple' decisions like where to live, vacation options, type of employment, and relationships with people?

These differences can result in serious conflicts, which can later cause heartaches and even breakups. Is that what you want in a relationship? I'm sure you do not! It is more critical than ever first to identify the things you want out of life.

As you complete this self-examination, the outcome prepares you to enjoy life with your soulmate. It also helps you see that choosing a soulmate goes beyond physical appearance and becomes more about what that person *brings to the table.'*

Many can't find their soulmate because they don't know what they want out of life. If you fall into that category, understand that you are not alone.

More than 50% of people looking for a soulmate are clueless about what they want from life. It is never too late to define the values that you appreciate in life. So what can you do?

Please take a moment to think deeply about

where you would like to see yourself in, let's say….5 to 10 years. Ask yourself the following questions:

- Where would you like to live?

- What places do you want to visit?

- How would you like to handle finances?

- How large of a family do you want?

- If health issues come up, what type of treatment would you want?

Your detailed answers to these questions will help you understand what matters to you in life. If you can answer these questions with specificity, you have just increased your chance of meeting your soulmate.

Ensure that you determine how the other person feels about these critical matters early in your next relationship before committing to the relationship.

Preparing for Your Soulmate by Knowing Yourself

Is there something special that someone should know about you that drives your happiness? This *something special* is not about your goals or how you view certain matters in life. It is about the characteristics that define you as a person.

Why is this important? Because if you know

yourself, you will know who can help you be a better person and who is capable of bringing out the worst in you.

Wondering how to do this? Ask yourself these soul-searching questions:

- What do you love doing?

- How do you spend your free time?

- What legacy do you want to be left when you are gone?

- What mistakes are you prone to make?

- How do you view others?

Asking these series of questions will help identify what makes you happy, sad, stressed, and fulfilled.

You can also buy a journal and jot down daily your reaction to the negative actions of others. You could do this exercise for a month and study the pattern. Daily, for a month, you can also list how you react to positive things you experience. This simple exercise will help you identify various facets of your emotions and how you respond to them.

Let's say that you notice that you are prone to react negatively to certain situations. In that case, it is best to work at controlling your response to negativity because controlling your emotions is vital to managing a healthy relationship.

Try to monitor your interests, temperaments, values, and activities. This personality assessment will help you get a clearer picture of who you are and how you react to good and bad news.

The final step to knowing yourself is to invite well-meaning family and friends to give you a sincere comment about who they perceive you to be.

Make sure you get only honest answers *(positive and negative comments)* from them, as you may not be able to improve yourself without it. You may realize that there are things about you that you need to adjust or change completely.

Apart from your family and friends, you can also ask work colleagues or your boss to tell you what things they feel you can improve. Realize that they may tell you things that you know are serious personality flaws. Thank them and work at improving any undesirable traits that they pointed out.

Understanding What You Need in a Relationship

Identify your views

Relationships are give-and-take unions with both parties satisfying the desires of the other. It is symbiotic rather than parasitic.

Do not feel that you need to exhaust yourself to make the other person happy while you feel dejected and abandoned. You indeed want a soulmate, but you are not desperate. Good things come to those who consistently work towards their goals.

While we will discuss patience later in this program, let us discuss legitimate needs in a relationship and how to identify your needs. Many go into a relationship without specifying what they need from a relationship.

Let me walk you through the process of determining what you need in a relationship. Remember, this is not related to the other person; it's all about what you want.

Grab a piece of paper and honestly answer the following questions:

- Do you want kids? If yes, how many?

- Are you a jealous type of person? Why?

- What tolerance do you place on cheating and marital infidelity?

- How do you view divorce?

- How do you view expenses and investing, and how should they be handled in the relationship?

While a common law in physics says: *"like poles repel and unlike poles attract,"* the opposite is the case when discussing personal needs in a relationship. Shared values count the most.

Similar values act as cement that binds the bricks of a healthy relationship. When you identify what you want in a relationship, it will be easier to focus on someone as a potential soulmate who shares those same desires.

Emotional needs

While your views are essential, emotional needs are desires that easily define the relationship's mood, whether happy or sad. It is vital to identify your emotional needs before you can find someone who can fill them.

Like you did earlier, grab a piece of paper and honestly write down your answers to the following questions:

- How much sexual intimacy do you need?

- When you explain yourself, how much value do you place on being understood?

- What value do you place on respect and being honored?

- How do you handle constructive criticism?

- When you are sad, what things make you happy?

Your answers to these questions determine who can fill your need for being your ideal soulmate, someone who can cater to these emotional needs.

Identifying your love language

Your *'Love language'* refers to how you receive love from others. In other words, what others do drives you to feel loved.

The 5 love languages are:

- **Words of Affirmation**: Saying things that make others happy

- **Acts of Service**: Doing things that make others happy

- **Receiving Gifts**: Giving other people gifts to show you love them

- **Quality Time**: Spending time with them to show you appreciate their companionship

- **Physical Touch:** Being physically close to others often involves a measure of physical romance

Which love language makes you feel loved the most? Your love language is another thing you must know before expecting someone to fill it. Different things touch our hearts, and it is natural to have a different love language.

Understanding your love language is easy; all you must do is analyze your current relationships with family and friends. The acts that make you feel valued the most are your love language(s). Those actions are what you should expect shown to you by a potential soulmate.

Just like you need to pack your bags the night before you embark on a journey, finding your soulmate starts with preparing your mind for a social journey.

This chapter has discussed various points that can help you prepare for love. Never expect that your next relationship will heal all hurt from your last relationship. Some have waited for years preparing themselves for their soulmate.

Spend time reviewing your personality because that is what you are *'bringing to the table'* in your next relationship. Commit to being a more attractive version of yourself. Remember, happy people attract happy people. If you are a better person, your probability of attracting a better person will increase.

Once you are ready for love, you need to know the types of people to avoid if you want to find your soulmate. That's the subject of the next chapter.

See you there in the next chapter!

CHAPTER 2: *'ATTRACTIVE-DEMONS'* THAT YOU SHOULD AVOID AND WHY THEY CAN NEVER BE YOUR SOULMATE

This chapter focuses on the type of people you should never consider as potential soulmates. I call them *'attractive-demons.'*

You might think that the list is common-sense and that anyone with a brain should know to avoid these people. Well, when you feel love, sometimes common-sense goes out of the window.

I want to reinforce in you that you must avoid attractive-demons. It can be challenging to stay away from a person who is a terrible match for you when they possess traits you find attractive.

If you date them, these attractive-demons will mess up your life and leave you worse than before you met them. As we go through each category of demon, note why you should avoid them. Recognize that this step is vital towards finding your soulmate.

With most people, what you see isn't what you get. They might look nice, they might speak well, but when you take your time to get closer to them, you realize that you should have never dated them.

So far, you know how to prepare your mind and soul, but what good will that preparation do if the person you are considering isn't lifelong material?

Even when you date a 'good' person, relationships can be challenging. When the connection is to an attractive-demon, it can do you more harm than good.

Such relationships will eventually end, and when they end, you'll be left dissatisfied and frustrated. Of course, no one expects perfection from their partner, but ignoring the attractive-demon warning signs will leave you emotionally stranded.

Let us examine 8 categories of attractive-demons that you should never consider for a soul mate and why you should avoid them.

Attractive-Demon #1: Psychopaths

A psychopath can be a very charming person. This person can work a room like a social butterfly and draw all attention to themselves. However, under the cover lay someone with a personality disorder who exhibits manipulative patterns when others are not watching.

Another type of psychopath is someone with antisocial behavior. Be careful about interpreting the word 'antisocial.' People generally think that someone who is reserved or keeps to themselves might be a psychopath.

Anyone can be a loner or reserved and be socially well adjusted. The word 'antisocial' refers to someone who deliberately goes against societal rules or norms just for their satisfaction alone.

Here are common signs you may notice in a person that might be a psychopath:

- Careless disregard for the safety of others

- General irresponsibility

- Consistent distortion of the truth for personal gains

- Lack of empathy and emotions

- Inability to differentiate right from wrong

- Lack of remorse when guilty

- Consistent violation of the rights of others

- Always breaking the law

Other symptoms might be risk-taking, being verbally abusive *(not always physical)*, and impulsive.

Why is a psychopath wrong for you?

Not every psychopath will turn out as portrayed in American movies as serial killers and rapists. The majority lead everyday lives, away from the spotlight. You will eventually find yourself frustrated having to deal with their consistent irresponsibility. It is best not to date one in the first place because the relationship will have no future.

Consider the negative points I just mentioned that you would have to deal with and then ask yourself, *"Is this the life I want with a soulmate?"*

Psychopaths are pathological liars. A pathological liar will stop at nothing to conceal whatever they are trying to hide, regardless of who they must hurt or what story they need to invent. They try to get what they want from you, even playing the victim card if necessary.

They will have strategically planned stories to gain your pity and force you to yield to them. Eventually, you will grow tired of their manipulations, and the relationship will end. Psychopaths always feel hurt when their partner fails to bend to them or accept their ideas. A psychopaths' response to rejection is often rage.

A psychopath will attempt to manipulate you every chance they get so that they keep exerting control over you. What is alluring about psychopaths is that they show a remarkable ability to protect.

They are fearless in the face of danger and show strength. These are great traits that some even confuse for showing love.

Attractive-Demon #2: Narcissists

A narcissist is someone who thinks that their worth is more significant than its actual value. In other words, they admire themselves for delivering value that they have not indeed delivered. They believe that everything revolves around them, even their partners.

While it's not wrong to attach some measure of importance to ourselves, we must understand the actual value we provide to others and not over-state it.

Once we over-state the value that we provide to others, it can turn into a mental health condition known as Narcissist personality disorder.

Once you prepare your heart and soul to attract a soulmate, you will meet many people. If you meet someone and they exhibit any of the following characteristics, you just may have encountered a narcissist.

- A sense of importance that seems beyond the actual value they provide to others

- An excessive need for admiration and attention

- A general lack of emotions like empathy and mercy for people

- Unstable interest in things

- A 'me first' attitude as if no one else matters

Again, narcissists lead everyday lives, and they seldom maintain long-term relationships. However, their partners have had to put up with the humiliating emotional conditions just because they were afraid to start a new relationship.

They might have other charming traits. In the beginning, you might mistake their narcissism for confidence.

Why avoid a narcissist?

Here is a scenario that might occur: You are out together for dinner, and while enjoying a well-prepared meal, you engage in some constructive conversation. A narcissist will try to dominate the entire discussion, making everything revolve around themselves.

You may start a discussion and reference an event that happened to you in the past. A narcissist will often relate that situation back to themselves. A narcissist tends to take everything personal, especially if you fail to compliment them or praise them for something they feel is praiseworthy.

According to a medical report, deep down, they

loathe themselves; thus, they need adulations, admiration, and praise from people to remind them of their imaginary amazingness. When they don't get that constant praise, respect, and attention, they flare up and get angry.

Another sign of a narcissist is their tendency to talk badly about past relationships. Remember that narcissists take things personally. They will complain that a past love interest failed to deliver either constant praise, attention, admiration, or even respect.

As you listen to people speak, notice what they say about others. If they formerly adored someone but now condemn them, chances are one day; it might be you that they condemn.

Attractive-Demon #3: Control freaks

A measure of control is healthy. You need to control some things in your life and how you react to your environment. But when a need for control becomes extreme, a deep desire to control others' reactions makes one abnormal and freakish.

A control-freak feels that things will go out of control, or their lives may fall apart without the power to control.

Control-obsessed people may not see themselves as control freaks. Requiring control over everything in life is psychologically unhealthy because many things in life are beyond our control, especially another human.

How to know if a person is a control-freak

While we may exhibit the characters to be discussed from time to time, a control freak tends to exhibit these traits all the time. One thing that shows someone is a control freak is an eagerness to correct a person when wrong.

They find opportunities to correct others, either involving little things such as pronunciation and spelling. If they were witnesses to a mutual event, they would find a way to update the account with their version.

When they notice bad manners, they are always the first to point it out. If a toddler misbehaves, they are quick to scold the mother or guardian. What stands out is that they often want to tell you that you are wrong.

This is due to the underlying perception that they are always right. If you ever get in a relationship with someone like that, imagine how detrimental that will be to your freedom of speech.

Another sign someone is a control freak is their eagerness to have the last word in a discussion or a sustained tendency to win an argument. They try to set arbitrary rules in a relationship and argue for any reason.

They believe that they know more than others and are always right. Narcissists and control-freaks have lots in common. A control-freak is usually a narcissist, but a narcissist is not usually a control-freak.

Control freaks are known for criticizing others. They judge every action and speech that may not agree with what they believe to be correct. They are usually opinionated and feel that people should do things their way. They are always difficult to convince, especially when it is clear they need to change their view. With them, the word 'team' stands for 'me,' and 'us' stands for 'I.'

They find it easy to disagree with others just to do so, but they respond with rage and anger when others disagree with them. In most cases, control freaks are hypocritical. If you are trying to search for your special someone, avoid control freaks.

Attractive-Demon #4: People with personality disorders

Everyone has their personality, way of behaving, thinking, and feeling, making them different from other people. Certain factors can affect a person's character; factors like background, culture, genetics, and environment.

A person is said to have a personality disorder if they behave, think, and feel in a way that deviates from what is generally acceptable.

Of course, psychopaths, narcissists, and control-freaks have personality disorders. Their personality often causes problems for others, and it is offensive to many.

If you want a soulmate, avoid people who are known to exhibit any of the following personality disorders:

- *Paranoid disorder.* This person tends to be unnecessarily suspicious of the intentions of others. They often mistake others' good intentions for evil motives, assuming people want to harm them.

- *Obsessive disorder.* They are obsessed with perfection and control. They pay too much attention to details and frustrate people around them.

- *Histrionic disorder.* These people feed on an excessive desire for attention. They are often clingy and nagging if not the center of attention. They can also become uncomfortable and jealous.

- *Dependent disorder.* They feel as if they cannot take care of themselves, thus excessively reliant on others. They find it hard to make simple decisions without help from others.

- *Borderline disorder.* They have unstable emotions and a poor self-image, needing constant reassurance from others. They have attempted suicide many times and are prone to self-injury.

- *Avoidance disorder.* They are extremely shy and often feel inadequate. When criticized, they feel hurt and are unwilling to mix and relate with people for fear of being rejected.

- *Schizoid disorder.* They often avoid social activities and find it hard to express normal human emotions.

Pursuing a relationship with any of the above-discussed personality traits will neither leave you satisfied nor fulfilled. The most reasonable thing is to avoid dating anybody with a known personality disorder.

Please note that some people may just be reserved and may not be suffering from any personality disorder.

Attractive-Demon #5: Momma's boy

How can I call a momma's boy an attractive-demon? Momma's boys are good men, kind and protective. Understand that dating them is no easy task because their mother controls their interaction with you behind your back.

What's the point of dating someone who is not ready to make decisions for themselves or tell their mother that she is wrong?

Falling in love with a momma's boy can be easy because of their kindness and concern for you. It's the same kindness and respect that their mother taught them to have for others. If you decide to carry on with such a relationship, expect the following:

- ***Undue comparison:*** They will often compare you to their mom. This comparison will be evident in small things like how you speak, act, clean, and even cook. You will experience many situations, telling you how their mother does things differently from how you just did it. Any attempt to convince them otherwise will fall on deaf ears because their mom is always right.

- ***Mom makes the decisions:*** Expect their mother's influence in any decision made. There is nothing that escapes mom's notice. Every time you both decide to do something, understand that mom already knew the issue before discussing it with you. There is a good chance that mom already decided, and the next move is to convince you that mom made the best decision.

  Mom will constantly meddle in your affairs, and every disagreement will pass through mom's ears for her analysis. Mom will also know about your sex life and all the kinky things you like doing and done to you. Let that sink in for a moment.

- ***Less 'alone' time together:*** Expect a significant number of dinners, vacations, holidays, and cold days with mom as the third-wheel. Expect mom to tag along during a considerable number of these moments that you wanted to bond with your partner. It will feel as if mom is always there, and she won't be shy about expressing dissatisfaction with anything you do or say. It will be like walking on eggshells around her.

- ***Mother is always right / you're always wrong:*** If you disagree with mom, you can be sure that the momma-boy will take mom's side and not yours. It will not matter if mom is dead-wrong. If there is anything mom could be right about, that will be the focus.

- ***Competition with their mom:*** You should not have to beg or clamor for attention in your relationship. But with mom in the picture, you will have to jostle for attention and affection. Imagine talking to your partner on the phone, and their mom calls; your partner will end your call to speak with their mother.

There is another problem: your partner wanting things done their way, like a spoiled baby. Remember that mommas-boys were babied from infancy, and their mom always satisfied them. You can expect that same rotten attitude from your partner in your relationship.

How to identify a mamma's boy

- If mom shows up unannounced even with keys and just opens the door

- If mom tells your partner how to dress, buys them clothes, and underwear

- Their mom fixes their problems, work issues and meddled in their past love life

- Mom still does your partners' household chores and laundry

- If you check your partner's call record and mom shows up 7-times out of 10-entries

- If mom does not appreciate you no matter how much kindness you show her, she may be jealous of you for taking her place in her child's life

- If mom is wrong, but your partner finds it difficult to stand up to her

As earlier mentioned, mamma's boys are good people, but having to compete with their mom frequently is a warning sign for you not to start a relationship with such a person.

Attractive-Demon #6: A person with too many friends of the opposite sex

I must speak exclusively to straight-people in this section. Some ladies prefer male friends. Understand one thing; men and women were not placed on this earth to be buddies. We were put on this earth to be sexually attracted to each other and have babies. That is our primal *(animalistic)* purpose in life.

Any male 'friends' that a woman interacts with feels either a romantic or sexual attraction for her. Either these guys want to date her long-term, or they just want lustful sex.

It's rare for any of these guys to want to be her brother figure or buddy. For this reason, if you date a woman with lots of male 'friends,' be prepared for these men to find fault in just about anything you do.

Any misunderstanding will be the guy up to evil. These 'friends' will seldom try to find ways to make the relationship stronger. Helping you build a stronger love works against their self-interest.

The same issues occur if a guy has too many lady friends. These lady orbiters want to find anything wrong with the woman in the guy's life.

If you start a relationship with a person who has too many friends of the opposite sex, it's like having too many hostile forces working against you.

These so-called 'friends' will hear about your relationship problems and offer solutions before you get a chance to influence the outcome. Is that what you want in a relationship?

You want a soulmate to give you the first opportunity to influence the direction of the relationship.

Attractive-Demon #7: Liars & Cheaters

At some point, we have all been untruthful, maybe to save face or to avoid troubles. However, liars are **ALWAYS** dishonest, aiming to deceive others just to stay safe. They have formed a pattern of lying, and people no longer believe them even when they attempt to speak the truth.

Cheaters are closely related to liars because their love interest never limits itself to you. When you see through them, they tell lies to get out of the situation.

Liars and cheaters are two categories of people you should avoid dating. For one thing, you will always doubt what comes out of your mouth; and not freely open to them. Love should be a free expression of your feelings.

Trust will also be hard to establish, and without trust, love cannot grow. You will always look for where their story doesn't add up because they have created a reputation for untrustworthiness. You want a love that you can relax into, not a love you must always doubt.

Here are warning signs that someone is a potential liar and/or cheater:

- They always hide their phone from you

- They never let you read their emails or messages on the phone

- Their story does not always add up

- They are found untruthful in little things

- They are known for flirting

If you notice several warning signs mentioned above in someone, you feel attracted to, save yourself the stress and avoid them.

Attractive-Demon #8: People who never admit their faults

Both parties must be ready to forgive the other for a relationship to thrive because it is easier to move past issues. To receive your partner's forgiveness, you must be prepared to admit your mistakes and apologize. A simple *'I was wrong'* or *'I am sorry'* can go a long way to soothe hurt feelings.

What if you are with someone who never accepts their mistakes? They believe that you are wrong, and they are always right! No matter how much evidence, they dogmatically insist that they are right and thus see no reason to apologize.

A failure to admit fault can put lots of strain on your relationship. It can even lead to breakups because if the situation persists, you start feeling less confident about your worth and abilities.

Even when you know you have done your best;

you still doubt your value. Just like with narcissists, an inflated feeling of superiority can be responsible for this. How will you know if the person falls into this category?

- When you make discussions with them, they insist on having their way

- When planning, this person never asks your opinion

- When they make mistakes, they justify their actions, perhaps shifting the blame

- Instead of apologizing when wrong, they remind you how lucky you are to have them

- They can't name a single thing that they did wrong in a past relationship

If you notice these traits, do not proceed with a relationship with this person. Avoid them because they can eventually ruin your self-image. In this chapter, I discussed the types of people you should avoid to find a soul mate. This step is challenging to follow.

People often hold back certain sides of their personality until you show your emotional commitment to them. At that point, your feelings may cloud any rational thought.

You must be strong to overpower your emotional feelings and get out of the relationship. Some may say that these personality types are clearly people to avoid, but now you have a checklist to refer back to as you date.

If the person you are considering falls within one or more of the personality types outlined, and you still move forward with the relationship, you can only blame yourself if things go badly.

Now that you know the types of people to avoid, you're ready to start the next step towards finding your soulmate; identifying ideal places you can meet your divine love.

Your divine love isn't going to pop out of your closet through some manifestation process. You're going to have to place yourself in front of humans, online and offline.

If you enjoyed this chapter about *'attractive-demons'* to avoid on your journey to finding your soulmate, you're going to love the next chapter about the best places *(and ways)* to meet your soulmate.

See you in the next chapter!

CHAPTER 3: THE BEST WAYS (AND PLACES) TO MEET YOUR SOULMATE

This chapter focuses on finding your soulmate once your mindset is ready to receive this person. You want to meet your special someone, but you cannot manifest this person with your thoughts alone.

You must put yourself in places to be discovered or where you can discover someone special. Must you attend every local event or join every online dating site before you meet them?

Well, not every local event and dating site, but as many as possible. I will touch on these methods because you must put yourself in the presence of people to meet someone special.

Understanding what you want in a soulmate

Finding your soulmate is not about finding just anyone. Your soulmate must be willing and able to satisfy your emotional and physical needs.

Some say that finding your soulmate is about finding someone birthed who amplifies your strengths and plugs the holes of your weaknesses. So how can you know if the person you feel attracted to is this divine person?

You want to look beyond superficial traits. While someone may be attractive and charismatic, you still need to go through the soulmate checklist you established earlier.

It takes time to decipher the person hidden behind gorgeous looks. You must spend time with them over a couple of dates. You also want to observe how they relate with others because how they treat others will eventually be how they treat you.

Take an objective look at them to see what their actions reveal about them. Keep your soulmate checklist in your mind as you meet people.

I do not believe in allowing fate to hand you a soulmate. You find a soulmate when you know what you want, and your eyes remain open for when this person crosses your path. If unsure of what you want in a soulmate, here are few things to look for and why they are necessary.

Does this person believe in you?

Everyone has dreams and life goals. These aspirations guide most decisions that we make in life. The reason for this is that everything we do is tied to our life goals. Your soulmate choice should be someone that supports you as you pursue your goals in life and not someone that deters you or slows you down.

Your soulmate choice determines the success of reaching your goals. Imagine dating someone that views you as a medical assistant when you view yourself as a surgeon.

This person cannot be your soulmate because they view your career differently than how you view it. If someone does not believe that you can achieve as much or more than you believe you can achieve, this person is not your soulmate.

Your potential soulmate should be your number one fan. When you make a mistake, they will show you how to recover, not criticize you, which can lead to a loss of self-confidence. In your journey to find a soulmate, make sure that you find someone who believes in you as much or more than you believe in yourself.

What effect will they have on you?

Your soulmate should bring out the best in you. When you are sad, they should be the reason why you smile. When your confidence is low, they should be that silent cheerleader urging you to push forward. You want a partner who boosts your emotions.

If all you think about is bitterness and anger when together and if your best days are being alone, these are signs that such a person is not the right one for you. The same way you expect this person to bring out the best in you, you must also be capable of bringing out the best in them. You both should shine better when together.

Your soulmate should also be someone who tells you when you are wrong or going down the wrong path. You do not want someone who agrees with you all the time.

You cannot improve if someone does not tell you hard truths. Evaluate each person you find attractive and ask yourself: *'Does this person bring out the best in me?'*

Will they put a smile on your face?

Is it love if you are not smiling? First, you must be happy before you can meet your soulmate. Your soulmate should amplify your happiness, and a great indication of happiness is smiling when you see them.

When you open the door or hold a video chat, does the sight of their face make you smile? When you are with this person, the atmosphere should feel electric. Even if they are not naturally funny, their presence must be enough to make you smile. They should make you laugh, even when doing everyday things.

In their presence, you should feel free to be yourself; childish, playful, or serious. When you are in a bad mood, they take you out of that emotional dungeon and make you smile again. If they cannot do these things, your soulmate may still be somewhere waiting for you.

Are they reasonable in times of disagreement?

A reasonable person reacts sensibly during times of disagreement. Why should you expect a sensible soulmate? The reason is that every decision they make reflects on you.

Others will project your partner's actions onto you, and in most cases, judge you by them. There are times you may not be able to think clearly for one or more reasons. If your soulmate is sensible, they will be able to make wise decisions on your behalf.

A reasonable person understands the value of yielding or acquiescing when necessary. It may be a decision that touches both of your lives.

If your partner is stubborn and insistent, decisions may benefit your partner more than you. A sensible soulmate is ready to compromise without hurting you or making enemies.

Does this person respect you?

Respect is defined as admiration for someone and their abilities or qualities. It can also be explained as due regard for the wishes of others or their rights. When learning about someone, notice how they react when you express your opinion.

Take mental notes of their reactions when you

make a decision that is different from what they would have done. Your observations will indicate if they respect you or not.

Consider their trustworthiness

They say that once in a lifetime, someone will betray you. When that comes from someone close to us, like your partner, the scar never heals. Before you get too emotionally involved, study this person well before starting a relationship with them.

Do they give you reasons to distrust them? Do they hide their mobile phone and other personal information? Do you feel that they are dishonest when disclosing their finances?

These are indicators that you should not ignore. Trust is a two-way street, so if you expect trustworthiness, you should be trustworthy yourself. After love and respect, trust is often regarded as the third most crucial quality expected in a soulmate.

They should have a forgiving spirit

As imperfect humans, one thing is familiar to us all: mistakes. If we do not stumble in actions, we stumble in words. When we offend, feelings get hurt, and tempers flare. If one does not course-correct quickly, grudges can fester and damage relationships.

Every relationship experiences occasional

disagreements. It may be as a result of something said or done. It could also be a result of something not said or not done. It might also be a result of a difference of opinion. While disagreements are unavoidable, one thing can help you both pull through no matter the issue: forgiveness.

Forgiveness is the art of overlooking ones' unintentional error because we value the relationship with that person more than our ego. Notice that I said 'unintended' error.

If someone hurts you without knowing, it is vital to have a forgiving spirit. If you date the wrong person, they may hold every mistake you make against you. A person who lacks a forgiving nature uses a person's errors to control them.

When you forgive, you do not preserve the action in memory to use against someone later. When someone holds onto wrongdoings, they keep every hurt feeling in a mental ledger that they open in the future.

They remind you of your unintended mistakes to manipulate and control you. A person who lacks a forgiving spirit finds it challenging to let go of what happened.

Take a moment to consider the person you find attractive. Do they have a forgiving spirit? If you make mistakes, will they use those mistakes against you? In their past relationships, has this person shown forgiveness for unintentional errors? Your soulmate should have a forgiving spirit. The success of your relationship depends on both of you having forgiving hearts.

Does this person show gratitude and appreciation?

Appreciation builds bonds. When someone passionately thanks you for your actions, it makes you feel appreciated. A quick thank you is never enough.

Appreciation is when someone looks you in the eye, touches you on the shoulder or hand, and verbalizes their gratitude for what you have done for them. The act could be your words or a deed. This appreciation motivates you to do your best to make that person happy.

On the other hand, an ungrateful person will not passionately give thanks. They might say 'Thanks,' but without any emotion behind it. An ungrateful person does not feel the energy that went into the good deed done for them.

There was no transfer of energy from them to you. You can never bond with an ungrateful person; therefore, that person can never be your soulmate.

What evidence has the person you have your eyes set on displayed to show appreciation?

They know how to show love

Love is so many things. It is the engine that drives a relationship forward; the cement that binds two people together; and the shield against forces that might try to damage a relationship.

Anyone you think could be your soulmate must know how to love because they have done it before. How will you know if someone can show love?

Consider the following indicators:

- They were loyal in a past relationship. If they stood by that person through hell and heaven. If they defended that person in that person's absence. These are clear signs of someone who knows how to show love.

- They do not hide their negatives. They show comfort in sharing their lives with you and the things they are going through.

- They are willing to help you in practical ways. Even if this help does not benefit them directly, they are eager to lend a hand.

- They take care of others: family, friends, co-workers. They do what is in their power to help others turn a bad situation into a good or manageable one.

- They listen when you express your viewpoint, even if that viewpoint contradicts their own. You can feel that they heard your opinion, even if they completely disagreed with it.

When you find someone that checks off this entire list, your soulmate could be stirring at you. Never settle for anyone that does not possess all these qualities.

Finding love when you expect it

While love will not find you while sitting at home thinking about it, you never know when you will find it, or it might find you. It is romantic to say that true love happens when you least expect it because it makes for a great romance novel.

Many people say that they did not plan to meet their soulmate and that it just happened. This characterization gives you the impression that you can sit at home, never surround yourself with people, and poof, love finds you while sleeping on your couch one day.

Consider what certified life and relationship coach Kelli Fisher said:

> *"When you are focused on meeting someone, the stress can be seen from a mile away........ When you do not have that at the top of your mind and are just enjoying yourself at the moment without any preconceived notions, things can progress*

organically".

Notice that she did not say to sit at home and think about love. She said to enjoy yourself while out in a social setting, then love can organically find you as you mix with people. Instead of focusing on meeting someone special every time you go to an event, focus on enjoying yourself.

Here are various things you can do that will place you in the company of people:

1. **Invest in your hobby**: We all have our hobbies. Maybe it is ice skating or going to the park to enjoy reading a novel. Whatever makes you happy, invest your time doing more of it to surround yourself with people.

   You should not invest in your hobby with the sole purpose of meeting your soulmate. You should do it to enjoy the activity. If your sole purpose is to meet a soulmate and you come home from each event not meeting this person, the disappointment can drain your energy.

2. **Make more friends**: If you enjoy meeting people, invest your time and resources in that. You could go camping with friends or hunting if that's what you love to do. You can meet other campers and hunters.

Do you enjoy reading or watching movies? Join a local book club or movie club. There will be lots to talk about after the event. Ensure that you have a love for the hobby and not just going to the event to find a soulmate.

3. **Re-evaluate your relationship checklist:** You have a set of qualities that you want in a soulmate. Earlier in this chapter, we reviewed qualities that should be on your list.

   From time to time, it is vital to re-evaluate this list. Why should you do that? Our desires change as we grow older. What you wanted in a partner 5-years ago may differ from what you want in a soulmate today.

   If you execute the steps outlined in this section, not only will you have more fun, but you position yourself to meet someone special. Focus on having fun at activities and let meeting your soulmate be a bonus.

   I will give you many more ideas on where you can meet more people who might be your soulmate. The more attractive you are as a person, the greater your chances of meeting someone when you least expect it.

Making a good first impression

The impression people formulate about you the first time they meet you never escapes their minds. Therefore, it is essential to make that first impression positive. Your first impression may be the key to unlocking that special moment when you meet your soulmate.

How can you make an excellent first impression? Here are a few ways to do it:

Dress and smell good

Please do not overlook the value of dressing well to find a soulmate. You do not need to wear tight clothing or show lots of skin.

Looking frumpy is not a good idea either. Regardless of your body's shape or physical weight, anyone can wear nice clothing that fits them well.

The point is that you want people to see you as someone who cares about themselves. Wear clothes with matching colors and patterns. Smell good with cologne or perfume, but not too much. One spray on the neck is all you need. Pay attention to your shoes and avoid color riots.

Be proud of where you are in life

Do not try to be someone you are not. If you are a high school teacher, say it with pride and not sadness in your voice. You attract the energy that you emit. If you want to attract a soulmate who has confidence, you must show confidence. Do not act rich when you are not.

Choose your words wisely

Be polite when speaking to others and compliment when appropriate. Let it show in your voice that you appreciate and value the opinions of others. When people are kind to you, express your gratitude generously and never be too shy to say that you are sorry when necessary. Your soulmate could be behind you, listening.

Talk about positive things in life; and not about how the world is screwed up; and that people are cruel; and that the government spends too much; and blah blah blah about the negatives in the world. You will only attract negative people to date, willing to complain as well.

Be mindful of your posture

Your posture says so much about how you view your life. You may not say anything, but your body language has a lot to say about you. When you speak to someone, they can tell if you have a passion for what you say.

Slouching is not an attractive look, and it only repels people. Even if your life is not going as planned, keep a positive posture to attract positive people.

Put your cellphone away when meeting people

If you speak to someone, you expect them to listen to what you say. When on your mobile device, people ignore you because you appear busy. When at events, you want to interact with people and look approachable.

To make an excellent first impression, put your phone away during conversations with someone. It shows that you value what someone has to say. Your soulmate might be the one speaking to you. It would be a shame if they viewed you as rude and walked away.

Trusting your intuition when searching for a soulmate

You might think that you do not have superpowers, but nature gave you intuition. There are times when you know something without being told or seeing anything. That is intuition, and many times, it is correct. Intuition involves listening to that inner voice as you analyze your next move.

Intuition is the highest form of individual brilliance because our innate feelings are usually correct. As you learn to harness the power of your intuition, you start to trust yourself more to make the right decisions.

There is another advantage of trusting your intuition. Intuition is always on your side, looking out for your best interest. Trusting your heart helps avoid unhealthy relationships with the wrong person. Here are things you can do to sharpen your intuition:

Avoid overthinking

Overthinking creates problems that do not exist and amplifies an issue beyond its current state. If you are not careful, this can negatively affect your intuition, causing it to give you mixed signals.

Let go of past trauma

Just as past traumas can change our outlook on life, it is vital to resolve in our hearts that we need to move on. If not, every intuition-trigger gets influenced by lingering thoughts of the past. When this happens, your intuition becomes less reliable.

Meditate more

Meditating frees your mind, taking your mind to a spiritual place. When you do not think rationally, spending time meditating will free your mind and reset your intuitive powers.

Pay attention to your body

What you feel influences your intuition. Control your emotions and avoid negative feelings like sadness, anger, and resentment. As you examine how you feel, you will know the best time to allow your intuition to make individual decisions for you.

Places to meet your soulmate

You can meet your soulmate anywhere and at any time. There are several great but unexpected venues where you can meet your soulmate. While this list is not comprehensive, it lists familiar places where you people meet people.

Offline places

Remember that your soulmate will not magically appear if you only think; you must also do- act and get out of the house as often as possible.

- Your workplace – You are at work 8 hours a day, maybe more

- In your neighborhood – If you live in an urban area, you probably walk to the grocery store, the cleaners, etc.

- At school – You can sign-up for classes at a local college and participate in study groups

- In the airport / On the plane – If you travel for work often, be open to people at the airport

- The gym – This is a great place to meet someone who shares a passion for health

- Public transportation – Maybe you take public transit to work; be friendly to people you see

- Volunteer – If you love pets or care about the homeless, you can join non-profit groups

- Religious center – Attending church also puts you in contact with people, and you can volunteer

- Local investment club – Another great place to meet people and maybe your soulmate

In all these places, you are visible to others. Once you build an attractive personality and style, you are positioned for your soulmate to find you.

Online places

You can also find true love online through online dating apps. Some of the top dating sites are easily found by using Google. Search for *'top dating sites'* and get a complete list. You might feel that online dating sites are filled with strange people.

That might have been the case years ago, but today you find the same caliber of people online as you find volunteering at non-profit groups or work.

If people were honest, I would bet that 70% of the people you see in church, at work, in the grocery store- all have online profiles on some dating site. Most people will not admit this fact, but more people are dating online and finding their soulmate than you realize.

Just register and set up a profile. Upload the best photos of yourself because your first impression will be your smile, your face, and of course, your body shape. Regardless of your body, you can wear the best clothing you have that gives you the smoothest look.

Online dating is more advantageous to people in their 50s, 60s, 70s, and 80s. I bet you did not know this fact. People over 50 are more serious about finding their soulmates.

If you are in your 20s and 30s, online dating can be more challenging because many of these people are just looking for a good time, not necessarily a soulmate. If you are in your 40s, finding a soulmate online can be a mix of serious connections and fun-seekers.

If you enjoyed this chapter about the best places to meet your soulmate, you will love the next chapter about what to do if you meet your soulmate at the wrong time in your life.

See you in the next chapter!

CHAPTER 4: WHAT TO DO IF YOU MEET YOUR SOULMATE AT THE WRONG TIME IN YOUR LIFE

Timing can work for or against you.

Meeting your soulmate is an experience most people want to have. In fact, many people yearn to have that deep-seated connection with someone, where they are sure that they are soulmates, destined by the universe to be together for life.

The thrill is exciting. Your soulmate has a way of making everything seem right. When they are around, the skies suddenly seem brighter. Their smile is the center of your world, and although you may not like it, it draws you in, and you are content to stare at them all day long.

With your soulmate, the connection is almost instantaneous. They feel the connection deep within just as you do, and if you are to have your way, you would want to seal the deal and get married to them immediately.

Your soulmate's appearance is usually characterized by nothing short of joy, happiness, peace, and contentment.

Although everyone (including you) prays to meet their soulmate, there are some conditions when being with your soulmate is downright impossible (or close to impossible).

One of these conditions is when soulmates encounter themselves at the wrong time. Just as with every other thing in the universe, timing plays a significant part in the subject of love and whether a relationship between soulmates will eventually blossom.

Let's take a quick look at the concept of *'meeting your soulmate at the wrong time.'*

What does *'the wrong time'* mean?

Back when you were much younger, *'the wrong time'* could mean many things in different situations. It could mean that it was past your curfew or that your parents may not have had the resources to purchase your 'ideal' birthday gift for you at the time. In any case, whenever it was not the right time for something, you were not going to get it.

This is the same thing that applies to the concept of meeting with and getting together with your soulmate. Although there is no curfew for you to keep to, you are not under the watchful eyes of parents and guardians who constantly remind you to make nice. Meeting your soulmate at the wrong time will, in most cases, lead to a lot of longing, pining, and loneliness.

In a nutshell, *the wrong time* in this context implies that although you have met your soulmate, the timing is not yet right, and for some reason, you will not be able to pursue and sustain the kind of relationship you are looking to have with them.

What constitutes *'the wrong time?'*

Now that you know that it is possible to meet your soulmate at the wrong time, you are most likely asking the question, *'how do I know that it is the wrong time?'*

Answering that question lies in understanding what constitutes *'the wrong time.'* Here are a few classical situations where you know that you have met your soulmate at the wrong time.

A. *Your soulmate may already be married*

And this news can wring your fluttering heart right out of your chest.

Imagine this scenario: You have always been a romantic at heart since young. You sit on the couch with a bowl of popcorn and a bottle of soda all night long-watching movies where the protagonists always win that special someone after all the hurdles they go through.

The last scenes of these movies leave you with

butterflies in your belly and a glimmer of hope that you, too, one day, will be like the protagonists in the movie - you will find your soulmate and walk with them into your happy-ever-after.

Although your friends scold you for doing so, you cannot seem to stay long in a relationship if it doesn't feel right. Sometimes, you avoid relationships and casual meetups with prospective partners only because you are waiting for the right one to come into your life and sweep you off your feet.

One day, when you least expect, you meet 'the One.' You feel yourself get flustered at the sight of them because you fit yourselves perfectly and make each other feel whole, just like pieces of a jigsaw puzzle.

They brighten your world, and you may even catch yourself a few times as you daydream about a happy-ever-after with them.

Your hopes shatter when you discover one day over coffee that the person you are sure is your soulmate is already married.

Although you are convinced that they feel the same thing for you as you do for them, a part of you dies as you learn that they are already entangled with another person for life.

If you are not careful, there is a tendency that you may throw caution to the winds and get involved in something you should not. You may start having an affair with the person, and often, this decision is fueled by your soulmate's proclamation to leave their spouse to be with you.

Meeting your soulmate at this time is dangerous because the connection that follows can lead you down the wrong path of making terrible decisions or leave you in a state of longing, pain, and angst.

B. ***Both of you may be fresh out of a bad relationship***

Not many people get out of a bad relationship to jump straight into a new one. And your soulmate may not make an exception because they met you.

When you meet your soulmate just after this person has just gotten out of a bad relationship, you may dislike them instantly. This is because although passion may exist between both of you, they may not be eager to pursue things with you.

Consequently, they may be nasty toward you, treat you with levity, or consciously get on your nerves. The reason for this is because they seek ways to get you out of their minds and maybe out of their lives for good.

They believe that if they can make you see them as a terrible person, you will dislike them, and your response toward them will change. They hope to take advantage of the dislike you will have for them to get you out of their minds and their hearts for good.

Although this may sometimes work, no rule says it must always work. However, meeting your soulmate at this time is hardly a walk in the park.

You may need to scale a lot of hurdles together, and whether both of you will be together ultimately dependents on the amount of work you are willing to put into the process of making things work.

C. Both of you may not be ready for anything "more"

"Someone can be madly in love with you and still not ready. They can love you in a way you have never been loved and still not join you on the bridge."

\-   Nayyiah Waheed.

Many people have at some point experienced this. After meeting with their soulmate and experiencing the thrills of finally getting to interact with the one for them, they get stumped because although they are sure the attraction is two-sided, their soulmate doesn't seem inclined toward pursuing anything more with them.

When you look deeper into the quote above, you will discover that it depicts another scenario when you can say that you have met your soulmate, but at the wrong time. This is arguably one of the most challenging *"wrong time"* situations because you may not be able to place a finger on the exact reason why your soulmate has refused to pursue anything more with you.

On the flip side, you may have met your soulmate - either professionally or personally. They may have come into your life as colleagues at work, a potential client you must work with, or just as a neighbor next door.

However, you may not be inclined towards them because you are not yet ready to be anything more than what you already are - platonic friends/acquaintances. This has happened to many people over time. In most cases, the result of this situation is that both of you may end up running around in circles for an exceptionally long time.

D. ***You may be married already***

This is just in line with the last point above. Meeting your soulmate after when you are currently married can be a challenging situation. This is not entirely unusual as there have been many incidents when this has happened to people.

When this happens, you experience the sparks and emotional high that comes with meeting someone who completes you in all obvious ways. Being around them is comfortable and rejuvenating.

You feel the mutual connection, and if you do not handle this correctly, it can lead to many challenges simultaneously.

For one, you may be tempted to move with the tides. This implies that you may throw caution to the winds and succumb to having an affair with them, especially if your marriage was already experiencing some challenges before this time.

When you meet your soulmate at this time, it may be impossible for you to be with them.

What to do when you meet your soulmate at the wrong time

After understanding that it is possible to meet your soulmate at the wrong time, you must know how to handle this if it should happen.

Understand that timing is everything in the game of love

Although this line sounds like a typical cliche, it is the absolute truth. Timing is everything in the game of love. The same way your parents may not get you that present you want for your birthday because they do not have the financial resources to (it was the wrong time), you may meet your soulmate at the wrong time.

This is what we have spent the last section of this chapter discusses.

Love is fantastic, and everyone wants to meet that one person for them. However, this connection may not lead to a happy ending if it happens at the wrong time. There are a few reasons why timing is vital in love and establishing a genuine connection with your soulmate.

- ***Finding your soulmate at the right time is vital if you're going to end up with the person you love.***

  If the four scenarios discussed in this section are removed from the equation, you will discover that it can be straightforward to build an enviable relationship with your soulmate; once you meet them.

- ***Finding your soulmate at the right time ensures that you do not go through the emotional pain that accompanies not being able to be with the one you love, even after you have met them.***

  Before you meet your soulmate, there is this longing in your heart. You want to meet that person who the universe designed for you and feel that the puzzle pieces have slipped into place. Meeting this person at the wrong time will only cause this longing to increase.

Now that you know they are there, it may be difficult or borderline impossible to stay away from them, and often, this leads to a lot of pain and heartaches.

- ***Meeting your soulmate at the right time is necessary if you do not want to make a mistake that you might regret.***

  Many people who have met their soulmates at the wrong time have made decisions they would not have made otherwise.

- ***Families have split because soulmates who met at the wrong time were unable to keep themselves from getting into an affair (if either or both were married).***

  Children must deal with the aftermath of their parent's separation after either of the parents met their soulmates at the wrong time. So, believing that your soulmate is out there and positioning yourself to meet them at the right time is a task you should undertake quickly.

- ***The knowledge that timing is everything can help you maintain a positive and upbeat attitude in the face of challenges.***

  Even when you may have met your soulmate at the wrong time, knowing that time can help reposition you to experience the love of a lifetime is enough to help you hold on.

  When you are about to be struck down with depressing thoughts that come from knowing that you have met your soulmate at the wrong time, remind yourself that the outcomes could have been different only if the timing was different.

You might have met them if they were not recovering from a bad relationship or going through a phase that will not allow them to be with you. With this knowledge, you can give them the time they need to recover from what is haunting them while still holding on to the faith that time can help you get together for real.

Count the cost

This applies to you the most if there are other people in the scenario except you. You may be married and have a family, and as a result, playing it by ear may not be an excellent solution for you.

There is every possibility that when you meet your soulmate, you may experience a rush of emotions that can overwhelm you. There is usually a passion between both of you, and sparks fly in all directions. The inability to handle these feelings usually results in bad decisions that affect many people in the end.

If you meet your soulmate at the wrong time in your life (especially if either of you are married), you may want to put your feet on the brakes and ask yourself a few questions, including:

- ***What is important to me right now?***

This will help you know the values you have placed in your life so far.

- ***Who are the important people in my life?***

  This analysis will reveal all the people in your life who you should consider before you decide to be with someone you believe might be your soulmate.)

- ***How will my decision affect them?***

  Honest answers to these questions will help you know how your actions will affect the people in your life.

  For example, it can reveal that although you may experience the thrill of something new, pursuing an affair with your soulmate who has come into your life at the wrong time may negatively affect your children in more ways than one, especially if they are still young).

When you go through this step, you will see that there may be sacrifices to be made in any case. For example, if you decide to pursue a relationship with your soulmate even when they are married; a broken home, bitter children, and a lot of persecution may result.

If, however, you decide to stay back and make things work with your spouse (if you are the married one), you may have to sacrifice that immediate pleasure for the long-term good of knowing that you were willing to stick it through till the end.

Before taking any step, please count the cost. If you think that the risk is worth it, you may go for it.

Seek professional help/guidance

This is one step you should take if you were already married or had a significant other in your life already before your soulmate came into the picture.

The decision to pull away from your marriage to be with a soulmate usually follows a season of intense marital challenges. If your soulmate steps into your life at the point where you are dealing with marital problems, there is every tendency that you will follow the promise and thrill that comes with them out of your present marriage.

However, before making this decision, you might be worthwhile to consult with a professional for help. This applies more to you if you feel that you still have a shot at salvaging your marriage or if there are already so many people in the equation (like young children).

When you and your spouse meet with a professional, they will help you in the following ways:

1. Decide if what you are feeling is worth going after.

2. Put things into perspective and count the cost associated with making such a big decision.

3. Analyze your marriage and see how you can make things work again. A professional will help you channel the emotions you are feeling towards your soulmate to your current partner, and this can be helpful if you are looking to make your marriage work, after all.

4. A professional can also help both your spouse and you through an amicable separation (if necessary).

In any case, a professional can help you navigate the boisterous season that follows meeting your soulmate at the wrong time.

Apply the brakes

This is necessary if you experience an insane level of attraction for your soulmate (especially if either of you are married). You are already getting emotional toward yourselves, and for this reason, remaining in contact may not be the best idea.

Observe the no-contact rule. The no-contact rule is that timeframe you spend away from your soulmate without trying, in any way, to contact them. During this period, you give yourself enough time to think, breathe, apply caution, and critically analyze the path you are on.

Taking time away from each other can be instrumental in getting your acts together and helping both of you make the right decisions for all the parties that will be affected if you're to continue without applying caution.

Trust the universe and allow time to work its magic

This applies when you believe there is a glimmer of hope in your situation. You may have met your soulmate when they are coming right out of a bad relationship or when they may not be in the mood for something more.

Under these circumstances, all you can do is know that time will help them heal and position them to be with you - if you really are soulmates.

However, do not entirely leave this to chance. Play your part in helping them heal (as much as they would allow you to) and take a few minutes to express to them just how genuine your feelings for them are.

You might want to make sure you let them know that you're in it for the long run, as this assurance can help them heal faster and hand your soulmate over to you.

Keep working on yourself so that timing can work in your favor

This applies the most to you if you have discovered that the things you need do not come to you when you need them. It could be an indication that you have not yet aligned yourself with the universe to get what you want at the right time.

This is not a time to despair, but a time to take the bull by the horn and get to work on yourself and your atmosphere; to make time work in your favor. There are a several things that you should make a practice of, including:

1. Start practicing the law of attraction.

The law of attraction is one of the foundational laws of the universe. In a nutshell, the law of attraction teaches that whatever you focus on and give more attention to grows.

When you apply this law in this context, it can imply that if you are constantly stressing out and you believe that you will not meet your soulmate at the right time, there is a good possibility that you may not.

To prevent this from being the case with you, begin to work on shifting your mindset from the place of stressing out over if you will meet your soulmate to the place of being convinced that you will meet them when you want to.

This way, you have a sense of being in control of your outcomes, and you will also reduce the chances of meeting your soulmate at the wrong time.

2. Position yourself to become that person to who your soulmate will be attracted to.

If you are looking to meet your soulmate and want to pursue something more with them, you should position yourself to become the kind of person your soulmate will be drawn to and who is ready to pursue something more with you.

To this end, you may need to take some time to heal from past hurts and trauma that can keep you in the same spot, even when your soulmate arrives on the scene. Also, applying the tips explained in the last chapter will help you prepare to meet your soulmate.

If you enjoyed this chapter about what to do if you meet your soulmate at the wrong time in your life, you will love the next chapter about signs that you have met your soulmate.

See you in the next chapter!

CHAPTER 5: SIGNS THAT YOU HAVE MET YOUR SOULMATE

Ignore this, and you may regret it.

So, you have spent your whole life waiting for the one. You have clung to faith, believing that against all odds, a day will come when you find the person destined to be with you.

You are not yet sure how that will happen, but one thing you know is that it must happen at the right time.

Here is the thing

You may have reached an inflection point where you have an idea of how things will pan out when you finally meet your Soulmate. All the movies you have seen and books you have read, create a picture in your mind's eye.

Your Soulmate is going to swoop in like royalty and save the day. When you finally meet this unicorn, the whole world will stop as you stare at their face and wonder how you survived all these decades without them.

But here is the challenge

While the picture I just painted may happen, no rule says it must occur the way I just described it. Several people who have met their soulmates and built enviable relationships with them did not have this experience.

If you meet these people, they will tell you stories of awkwardness that accompanied their first meeting. These stories go on to prove that there might not be a release of rose petals falling from the sky when you meet your Soulmate.

And if you ignore this fact, you may miss out on connecting deeply with your Soulmate even when you have met them.

This is what this chapter aims to help you achieve. To answer a salient question; *"how do you know that you have met your soulmate (when you eventually do)?"*

How to know that you have met your Soulmate

Here are some things that you will notice when you meet your Soulmate. These serve as indicators that you have met your Soulmate.

A. **Your Soulmate will speak your love language**
Before going any further, I need to examine the

concept of *"love languages."*

A language is a medium of communication that touches your soul. It serves as a means through which one can make their intentions known to another.

Similarly, *"love languages"* are the media through which we communicate (give and prefer receiving) love. A love language demonstrates how a person expresses love to himself and another.

Generally, there are five love languages, and these include:

1. Words of affirmation

People stimulated by this love language want and value verbal communication as an expression of love. They want their partners to remind them repeatedly through words that they love them.

Telling someone you love them with passion matters most. Merely uttering the words will have no significance. People who fall into this category are pretty vocal about their need for love. When they fall in love, they do not hesitate to bear their hearts and communicate what they feel for their partners with their words.

2. Physical touch

If this is your love language, you will discover that you feel happy when your partner does more than vocalizing their feelings for you. People with this love language value a passionate touch but non-sexual, and they do not hesitate to return the favor.

If your partner's love language (or one of them) is physical touch, they find it easy to give you a massage after a stressful day or rub your knee with one hand while they steer the car in with the other hand.

3. Service

People with this as their love language do not just want words that express how much they mean to their partners; they want to see these words in action. As Janet Jackson said in her 1986 song, *"What Have You Done For Me Lately?"*

They want their partners to convert their love for them into deeds. To these people, the smallest acts mean more than many words. The more recent the deed, the more feel your love.

If your love language is service, you will discover that you feel exhilarated when you find out that your partner handled the grocery shopping just to let you have some more time for self-care. Service in this context does not mean that you will subjugate your partner.

However, you want them to take things past the

verbal *"I love you"* and perform actions that depict them in that light. Something as trivial as washing the dishes, doing the laundry, and taking the dog out for a walk makes a world of difference.

4. Quality Time

If your love language is quality time, you want your partner to consciously try to be with you if they genuinely love you.

People with this as their love language are big on having couples' hangouts, spending time together chatting, seeing movies with themselves, and so on. People of this category cherish their partners' full and undivided attention when together.

Turn off the cellphone and focus on your partner if quality time is their love language. Fiddling with your phone, returning a text, reading a book does not count as quality time just because you are in the same room together. Make your partner the number 1 focus for a few hours.

5. Receiving gifts

People who value this as their love language, love it when their partners give them gifts, no matter how trivial the gifts may seem. It could be a flower, chocolates, or just the gift of consciously trying to spend time with them.

If this is your love language, you may find yourself expecting and demanding gifts from your partner. If they cannot get you the things you require, you may slip into a mindset where you believe that they are uninterested in you and do not love you as they claim.

With these love languages explained, the first way you can know that you have met your Soulmate is that this person will speak your love language almost immediately.

Quickly, they read and understand cues that suggest your love language, and they slip into the mindset where they speak your love language. They do not see doing this as a favor to you or as a burden that they must put up with for the rest of their lives.

So, if you are at that place where you are not entirely sure whether the person in your life is your Soulmate, you may want to assess this factor. Be careful, however, not to base your decisions on this factor alone.

You must consider some factors in addition to this, and I will examine them in the next points.

B. Your life goals align

They are called your "soulmate" for a reason. This is because, amongst many other things, your Soulmate should have the same goals as you and be headed in the same direction as you. This factor is critical in your journey to finding and sticking it out with your Soulmate.

When assessing the person that you believe to be your Soulmate, there are critical questions you must ask. They include:

1. Do you both have the same goals in life; financially, professionally, and spiritually?

2. Are you both passionate about the same things; hobbies, politics, personal growth?

3. Are both of your visions aligned; 5 years from now, even 20 years down the road?

Your Soulmate should inspire you to live a life beyond where you currently breathe. This person's goals, vision, and purpose must align with yours. This is how you will help yourselves grow and become better as time progresses.

C. There's a sense of calm whenever you're around them

You should expect this one thing when you interact with that person you believe to be your Soulmate.

Your real Soulmate makes you feel at ease, and when you are with them, you know peace, calmness, and contentment like never before. All of your problems seem to melt away when your eyes make contact.

Many times, this happens as an unconscious thing. Although they may not purposefully try, they make you feel at ease when you occupy the same space. As a result, you love to be with them, and spending time in their company makes you more than just happy, but at peace with the world.

D. Your heart says yes

Let us not brush this point under the carpet because this is one of the first things experienced when you meet your Soulmate. The same way you have a deep feeling that you will get that job offer and it happens just that way is how this works.

When you meet your Soulmate, there is something about them that draws you in, and you have that assurance that they are the one for you.

When it comes to this matter, do not downplay your feelings' importance because your heart will tell you if you are with the right person. When you wake in the morning, everything about this person feels right, in alignment, and destined for success.

E. You complement yourselves

This is one of the necessary tests for knowing if they are your Soulmate. When you find your Soulmate, you discover that they perfectly match you in terms of the fact that they balance you out. Your Soulmate is a compliment for you in many areas; they complement your emotions, behaviors, and your dreams.

This is important because often, you will not be the same as your Soulmate. You both may be polar opposites in many ways, but those differences feel like something to learn from, not something to avoid. You will not have the same temperaments or behave the same.

However, in the things that matter, your Soulmate will compliment you.

For example, their cool-headed nature complements your spontaneous one or vice versa. Perhaps you love to spend money and need someone even-handed and rational to cool your excitement to spend it all but to instead save and invest.

F. You challenge yourselves

Your Soulmate challenges (not pushes) you to greatness, which brings out the best in you. A challenge is a small poke, passive-aggressive in nature. A short statement like, *"I have seen you create a better one before,"* is a little poke to do better.

The person moves to another discussion after commenting. They do not keep drilling the point, and if they do, now they are being pushy.

They challenge you to reach for your dreams and aspire you to become so much more. With your Soulmate, there is no unhealthy competition. Instead, they believe that whatever you may be doing now is only a fragment of the things you can eventually do.

As a result, they consistently challenge you to take up more significant responsibilities, smash bigger goals, and grow while you are at it. This results from the fact that your Soulmate is committed to your growth in all aspects of your life.

G. **Your Soulmate will not give you up quickly**

Let's face it. Relationships aren't usually roses and jelly beans. A time comes in every relationship that appears as though everything has gone to the depth of hell. At these points, one can either pack up and leave the relationship (which usually seems like the easy solution) or remain in the relationship and fight to preserve it.

Your relationship will not be an exception to the rule. No matter how much you love your partner, a time will come when you begin to experience these *preserve love or die trying'* moments.

A sign that the person you are with is your Soulmate is that they will not give you up when these challenges appear. Your Soulmate possesses a history of sticking with rocky relationships instead of throwing in the towel and moving on with their lives.

When they speak about past loves, they talk about how much they tried to make wrongs right and how it pained them to walk away eventually. Your Soulmate is no fool and knows the value of their love and time.

H. **The chemistry is undeniable**

This is another litmus test that reveals that you have met your Soulmate. Soulmates who have connected with themselves often admit that they had chemistry, which in some cases was almost instantaneous. This matters to you if you are big on the physical stuff in your relationship.

You will most often notice that you may find it challenging to keep your hands off yourselves when you meet your Soulmate. The best part of this is that the feeling is usually not one-sided.

I.   You feel secure in your relationship

When you are with your Soulmate, there's no need to feel insecure. This is because your Soulmate complements you, which implies that you are skilled in different ways. As a result, when you are with them, you feel secure.

There is usually no need to feel jealous or threatened by your Soulmate, and they make you feel safe when you are with them.

J.   You feel a strong sense of empathy toward them

You are touched by what happens in the life of your Soulmate. This is not some form of distant relationship where you can go your separate ways for months on end without keeping in touch with them. With your Soulmate, you are empathic, and the things that matter to them matter to you as well.

The connection between your Soulmate and you is one that is strong, such that whatever makes them happy makes you happy. When they experience discomfort, you are sad. When your Soulmate achieves something worthwhile, you feel it as though you were the one that championed the win.

K. You can be real with your Soulmate

Most people have a way of putting on a facade when they are with people. They feel as if they cannot be their authentic selves with people for some reason. This usually results from a fear of judgment or misunderstanding or the need to prove a point.

However, this is not the case with your Soulmate. When you are around your Soulmate, you find that you can be yourself with them. Your inner-dork emerges, and it feels good to let your dorky side shine at times.

You do not fear judgment from them. You can be entirely honest with your Soulmate and not afraid that they will judge you or make you feel stupid.

Your Soulmate is that person you can confide in without the fear of having your deepest secrets revealed to the world.

Although you may be skilled at showing people what you want them to see, your Soulmate can get you to be completely honest with them and yourself as well. You do not mind being vulnerable around your Soulmate.

L. You attach a sense of purpose to your Soulmate

Your Soulmate's entry into your life opens you up to another definition of purpose. When you meet your Soulmate, there is just this part of you that keeps reminding you that you did not only meet them because you wanted to or because you orchestrated the meeting.

Your Soulmate's entry into your world is attributed to powers beyond you. The universe and the laws of nature work as a team to place your Soulmate in random locations.

As a result, you value your relationship with your Soulmate greatly, and you would not treat them like they are just anyone else in your life.

M. Sometimes words are not needed

One of the main ingredients of a successful relationship is that there is unhindered communication between the partners. This is the same with the relationship you have with your Soulmate.

The only thing is that this time, the communication in the relationship you have with your Soulmate is much more than just words.

When you are with your Soulmate, this sense of alignment seeps into your subconscious. The more you append time with them, the more your minds become attuned to themselves. At some point, words will not be entirely necessary.

This is the point where your Soulmate understands your gestures and facial expressions and may even be able to complete your sentences for you. At this point, you begin to sound alike, and your communication happens on an even deeper level.

N. Their past relationship will not hurt the future you can have with them

Almost everyone has had their share of challenges in the past. Your Soulmate is not an exception to this. They may have had terrible relationships in the past and been through hell and hot water.

However, when they are with you, they put past negatives in the rearview mirror and allow the past to remain where it should be - in the past.

Your Soulmate will not lay the pain of past hurts at your feet. Whatever pain they experienced with past lovers does not seep into their relationship with you.

They treat you as a new beginning. Allowing you space to show your uniqueness. This is one thing that makes a relationship with your Soulmate different from the relationships you may have had in the past.

How to know if what you felt was true love

This is a topic I must do some justice to before we wrap up this chapter.

Many people have different definitions of true love. To some, true love means that the other person must be all and about them. Some people believe that their word must be law, and when they get into a relationship, they go in with this mindset.

On the other hand, some people believe that true love is all about the relationship's physical aspect. To them, their partner does not love them if they do not experience sexual penetration several days each week.

Are these true? We will find answers to this in this section of the chapter. Knowing if what you felt was true love is instrumental toward helping you understand if the relationship you are wishing will bud is worth it after all. So, here are a few signs which reveal whether what you felt was true love or not.

A. You can't bear to see the other person hurt

This is one of the first things you must consider when you are beginning to ask if you feel true love. True love cannot bear the thought of the person that it is directed toward getting hurt or dealing with pain alone.

True love is quick to take up the pain the other person feels and stops at nothing until the person it is directed at begins to heal. If what you felt was true love, you would have had this experience.

B. True love thinks long-term

When you get into a relationship with someone you feel true love for, you will discover that you think of them in the long-term. You are not just with them to kill time and have fun when bored.

You see them as part of your future, and you relate to them in that same way. As a result of this, they are a significant part of your life. You include them in all the significant decisions of your life, and you are serious about what you feel for them.

C. Their opinions matter to you

When you feel true love toward a person, you do not treat them as insignificant or as if their opinions do not matter to you. When you are about to make a decision, you think of them and what they would say about the action you want to take.

You actively seek them out and communicate your thoughts with them, after which you are vocal about wanting to hear what they have to say.

If what you feel is genuine love for them, you consider their opinions and take actions that will not hurt either of you in the end.

D. You are careful about making promises and you keep your words

Not keeping your words in a relationship is a

precursor for distrust. Distrust will ultimately sever any relationship until the parties involved get tired and go their separate ways.

One way to prove that what you felt for someone is true love is that you are incredibly careful of the promises you make to them because you have a commitment that you will keep true to all the words you have said to them.

When you make a promise to someone you feel true love for, you intentionally adhere to your promise until you have accomplished what you said to them. This is because you feel strongly for them, and you do not want the distrust associated with making promises and not fulfilling them.

Being in a relationship with your Soulmate is exhilarating. It promises thrills like nothing you have ever known. Knowing what to look out for will help you identify your Soulmate when they eventually come into your life.

I dedicated this chapter to revealing signs that you have met your Soulmate. Pay attention to all fourteen signs discussed in this chapter if you do not want to experience the regret that comes with realizing that you found your Soulmate after losing them to life and chance.

The signs discussed in the last section serve as a pointer to whether what you are experiencing is true love.

If, after your analysis, you discover that you are not feeling true passion for the person you are with now, this is an indication that they are not your Soulmate after all.

If you enjoyed this chapter about how to know if you have met your soulmate, you will love the next chapter about how to make love work for you.

See you in the next chapter!!

CHAPTER 6: HOW TO MAKE LOVE WORK FOR YOU

Newsflash: You must work daily for love to succeed!

So now you have met the love of your life. After waiting all these years, you have finally found the one who makes everything in your world seem brighter and the world a better place for you. You have met them, and you can tell with everything in you that the wait was worth it in the end because this person fits you perfectly.

With butterflies in your belly and the giddy feelings of happiness you have around them, you believe that it will all be a game of love and happiness forever. You do not expect that things can turn sour at some point.

One day, you argue with your soulmate, and after those heated minutes of anger, you relax on your comfortable couch with a bowl of popcorn in hand. While you mull over the activities of the last few minutes, you cannot help the shock that races through your spine.

You never believed it could happen this way

You never thought it would get to a point where you will feel so angry with your soulmate that you do not even want to see them again, at least, for a while. And that is where the problem begins.

As much as the idea of a soulmate who understands you to the latter and would not give you any trouble at all seems beautiful, it almost would not happen to you on a whim. Even after you have met your soulmate *(and you are sure that they are the one)*, your relationship with them cannot be free of hurdles and bad days.

Love works and is beautiful, but the beauty is only for those who understand this thing; fairytale love hardly ever exists. Every love story with a happy ending *(including yours)* is entirely dependent on whether the parties involved are true to themselves.

The relationship hinges on the ability to stick it out and a willingness to fight for the bond they share and know that it may take a lot of work to get the beautiful ending desired.

In a nutshell, love is not a programmable robot that works independently. Love is life, and to make it work for you, you must treat it as such; with care, the needed attention, and the determination to make it work for you.

That is what this chapter will be dedicated to;

helping you make your love and relationship with your soulmate work out for the best.

What you must know if your relationship with your soulmate will be amazing

Although they are your soulmate and you feel this deep connection with them, there are things you must know to have a tremendous and blossoming relationship with them.

Over the years, many people have ignored these and thought that they are not necessary. Many others have dismissed them as old wives' tales and thought them to be of no relevance in one's relationship with their soulmate. The result of these thoughts is that although these people end up meeting their soulmates, they are unable to pursue and maintain a healthy relationship with them.

If they are unable to manage these, things that are supposed to be loving and beautiful relationships can quickly deteriorate into toxic and terrible relationships, with the two people who are supposed to be soulmates hating themselves with a fiery passion.

To avoid this from occurring, there are things you must know about your relationship with your soulmate. Pay attention to the following:

Your soulmate is human, just like you

The concept of finding your soulmate has become skewed over the last few decades, with people believing that they will find their soulmates and discover that they have hit the jackpot and found someone free of human flaws.

Well, unless you plan to date and spend the rest of your life with a ghost or an angel of sorts, this one mindset hack will help you set yourself up for a loving and beautiful relationship. The knowledge that your soulmate is human as well will do many things for you. It will help you:

1. Get rid of unnecessary and exceedingly high expectations in the relationship.

Many people crash and burn in their relationships because they have high and unbelievable expectations of the other person. Knowing that your soulmate is a human, too, will help you make room for their flaws and understand that although they may have your best interests at heart (at all times), they may fall short of your expectations from time to time.

2. Get prepared to forgive them in advance.

This point is in line with the one above. You have come to know that your soulmate will fall short of your expectations and may even hurt you sometimes *(although unintentionally)*, you can begin to prepare yourself for those times. One way to get ready is to prepare to forgive them in advance. It will not be easy, but it will be worth it in the end.

3. Become more attentive to them as well

When you realize that your soulmate is human, you become more conscious of them than you would have if you were to treat them like an apparition that fell out of the sky or a robot sent by the universe to satisfy your every whim.

The knowledge that your soulmate is a person as you are will help you remember that they have emotions just like you. Some things irritate, excite, annoy, or make your partner happy. Armed with this knowledge, you can look out for the things they like and play your part in making them happy for as long as your relationship lasts.

4. Challenges will come up as you journey towards building the life of your dreams

As much as this is one thing that many people run away from, failure to confront it head-on does not change the fact that it is the truth and nothing short of that.

As you get on with building an enviable

relationship with your soulmate, be aware that a time will come when things will not be as rosy as you may have expected. You may experience a rough patch along the way.

If you cannot conceive these ideas in your mind as you get into a relationship and have a contingency plan in place ready, you may give up at the first sign of resistance.

5. *You must be committed to getting to 'happily-ever-after'*

Well, that is if you want your relationship with your soulmate to end up in a 'happily-ever-after' state.

The 'happily-ever-after' state is one thing that many love stories have been able to document and display over time; the hurdles those in love must go through to get a shot at the lives they want in the end. Borrow a leaf from these stories even as you venture into a relationship with your soulmate.

As much as you may not want to hear this, life may not let you have your soulmate and experience a happily-ever-after without throwing you some curveballs. The universe will test you before you can have whatever you desire. One of those tests you will have to pass in your relationship with your soulmate is the ability to stick it through till the end. One easy way to achieve this is by making a list of all the worst-case scenarios.

What are the things that can go wrong in your relationship with your soulmate? Brainstorm these possible situations and begin to create a way to weather them together.

The idea is not to bail at the sight of the slightest challenges but to be the soulmate who will stick close and help them through their darkest times.

What you need to make love work for you

Making love work for you is something you should have at the top of your mind right now. This is because you will only truly be happy when you have found your soulmate, proven to the universe that you are meant to be together, and you get to start building the 'happily-ever-after' of your dreams.

However, to make love work for you, there are some skills that you must possess. Skills are not only needed when you are looking to start a new job or establish a new business to get the bucks rolling in.

To have an enviable relationship with your soulmate, you need a plethora of soft skills. This section takes a quick look at these skills and where they are necessary for your relationship.

1. Communication

Communication is more than the lifeblood of every relationship, and your relationship with your soulmate is not exempted from this. Suppose communication is absent or stilted in your relationship.

In that case, it is only a matter of time before your relationship hits an iceberg and is submerged under the boisterous water called life.

The function of communication in any relationship cannot be overemphasized. Here's why communication is necessary for your relationship.

A. Communication helps you establish a connection with your soulmate in a way nothing else can.

This is because when you communicate *(verbally and non-verbally)* with your partner, you open yourself up to them and allow them to know what is happening with you in real-time.

This way, your soulmate can help you when you desperately need it and can also be there when you need someone to be happy with.

This one key will strengthen your relationship tremendously; the ability to communicate effectively.

B. Communication helps you make the best

decisions in your relationship.

When your soulmate is transparent with you about the things they like or do not like, you can experience them in a way that they love. This way, you do not set them off or trigger unfavorable responses in them toward you. The same thing happens when you return the favor.

C. *Communication eliminates suspicion and distrust in any relationship.*

When distrust, suspicion, and paranoia begin to seep into a relationship, a partner starts to feel like the other is withholding something. The danger with this is that when it happens, there is every tendency that the other person's mind can take advantage of the darkness it is in to create ambiguous pictures and make a molehill appear as though it is a mountain.

The result is that if left unattended, the relationship can hit the rocks at any time as the people in the relationship begin to feel estranged from themselves. This can happen to you even if you are in a relationship with your soulmate.

To prevent this from taking place, make it a point of duty to communicate effectively with them. Are they having a bad day? Talk to your soulmate. Are they feeling frustrated about something or someone? Hear them out without offering solutions. You do not always need to fix a problem; try to absorb the feelings of the person experiencing the pain. Even if there's good stuff happening around you, tell them.

For the sake of your relationship's health, never leave your soulmate in the dark. Also, in the spirit of communicating, carving out time to spend with them and giving them your full attention is also a form of communication.

2. Remembering the small things

While this may be subjective and depends on your interpretation of what matters to you and what does not, remembering the small things in any relationship is one skill that can make all the difference.

Something as little as remembering that your soulmate loves their coffee with a bit of cream in it, or the day they got their first contract and celebrating it with them, can show them that they are essential to you.

This has a way of going beyond the usual *"I love you"* and *"You are special to me"* chant that everyone seems to drop on their partner sooner or later. It reiterates the fact that if you can remember the tiny things about them *(especially the things that matter to them, like their favorite color or best meal)*, it means that you pay attention to them.

Remembering the small things in your

relationship is one way to tell your soulmate that they are essential to you, deserve your undivided attention, and that you are not afraid to make them feel special any chance you get.

3. **Knowing the magic words and when to use them.**

We established in an earlier section that relationships will not always be easy. Notwithstanding how much you try to, there will always be those times when you may have differences with your partner. These are the times when this skill is needed.

For a relationship to work, both parties must make it a point of duty to know when to get off their high horses and allow themselves to be vulnerable for the long-term safety of their relationship. Pride and healthy relationships have never been two peas in a pod and never will be.

And an expression of satisfaction is the inability to identify and effectively use the magic words; *"sorry,"* *"thank you,"* and *"please."* As small as these words seem, they play a significant role in any successful relationship. Here's how they work.

A. "Sorry": A perfect way to use this is in the sentence "I am sorry." It shows that you know that something has happened in a way that it should not have. You are taking responsibility for it, and you are willing to do better. This is one way to get your soulmate to forgive you even when you make the mistakes you are bound to make in the relationship. Many relationships have gone south because neither person understood this nor did their best to follow through.

Apologizing can take a lot of courage. It suggests that you understand that you have made a mistake, and doing it requires that you get off your high horse.

However, the dividends of knowing when you are wrong and taking the responsibility of apologizing to your partner are immense. Imbibing this character is one way to make sure that your relationship lasts an exceedingly long time.

B. "Thank you": Using this phrase implies that you are appreciative of a kind gesture and that you do not see it as something you had the right to.

Thank you is a sure sign that you are not battling with an entitlement mentality. It is an acknowledgment of the efforts of your soulmate in your relationship.

To build a healthy relationship with your soulmate, you must express appreciation for any and everything - no matter how small it might appear. Vocalizing your appreciation by the proper use of the words "thank you" can go a long way to help you maintain a healthy and happy relationship.

C. "Please": This is also another word that shows that you aren't battling with the entitlement mindset. Many people do not use this word often, and it is a reflection that they think/believe that their wishes should be their partners' commands. If you do not make it a point of duty to communicate to your partner that you are soulmates *(and you do not intend to use them as some form of cheap help)*, you may want to incorporate this word into your vocabulary for everyday use.

4. Understand your partner

We established in an earlier section of this chapter that although you are getting into a relationship with your soulmate, you must consciously remember that they are humans as well.

In line with that, when you have come to terms with the fact that you are in a relationship with a person that you love, it is your job to understand them. Look out for these points if you want to have a successful relationship.

A. Understand their

personality/temperaments.

Your soulmate's temperament is a significant part of your relationship, and understanding it is vital. Since your partner's temperament is a huge part of their entire personality, you may want to spend time to figure it out.

When you have understood their temperament/personality, you can figure out how you complement yourselves.

B. Understand their boundaries

All of us have those lines we have created in our lives; invisible lines that no one can cross. To keep enjoying your soulmate, you may want to take out time to understand their boundaries.

What things make them tick and get them emotionally excited? What are the things that they love, hate, and most of all, the things that they find revulsive?

When you have answered these questions, you can make better decisions that concern them and position yourself to be the partner they want to be in a long-term relationship with.

C. Their love language

In an earlier chapter, we discussed the five love languages. As you journey toward building an enviable relationship with your soulmate, you must understand their primary love language.

This knowledge will help you communicate your love for them in a way that they can easily understand, interpret, and cherish.

Trying to express love by giving only gifts to someone whose primary love language is 'words of affirmation' may not carry the same weight as it would if you are to say the magic words to them again.

5. Consciously work on your love until it grows to become something sustainable

Love is more than the emotions and fluttery feelings that come with finding your soulmate the first time. If you are to grow your relationship into something worthwhile and stand the test of time, your love and feelings must become sustainable.

The question in your head is, *"how do you achieve this?"* Allow me to give you a few pointers.

A. Pay attention to making sure that your needs are met

And by *"your,"* what is meant is the both of you. You must pay attention to your soulmate and ensure that you meet their needs on all levels; physically, emotionally, mentally, and in all areas.

They must also commit to doing the same thing for you. As your relationship progresses, your soulmate must become the person to whom you run to when you have a challenge and need help.

When you begin always to seek the support and attention of someone who is not your soulmate, it may be a sign that your relationship may already be in some trouble.

B. Focus on respect and make sure this goes both ways.

For any relationship to flourish, both parties must be intentional about mutual respect. It is practically impossible for a relationship to last for a long time if one party makes it a point of duty to be at the receiving end of all the love, attention, and respect without giving back.

We have established the fact that your soulmate is a human as well. The way you want to be respected is the same way you should make it a point of duty to return the favor to your soulmate. When the relationship has both of you respecting yourselves and each other's ideologies about life, it will last for much longer.

C. Do not be ashamed to be vulnerable with your soulmate

Although you may project yourself as a strong

person who cannot be moved by anything, this should not be your focus in your relationship with your soulmate. When you seek to get to your *'happily-ever-after,'* you must make it a point of duty to consciously make yourself vulnerable to them.

Let them see the real you that you do not show the rest of the world. This will help inspire confidence and trust in you, even as they do the same for you.

D. Establish passionate communication

This goes beyond having shallow conversations with your soulmate. Passionate communication is vital to secure your relationship and ensure that you end up in the *'happily-ever-after'* you seek.

You must feel something during, and after each time you communicate with your partner, they must also feel that energy. If you or your partner feel nothing powerful after 'communicating,' then you never truly communicated; you both merely spoke to each other.

Train yourself to confide in your soulmate. They need to be aware of all the details of your life if they are to stick with you and be with you in the relationship for the long haul. Communication is vital to ensure that doubts and suspicions do not take root and destroy your relationship as it unfolds.

The benefits of communication in a relationship have been outlined in an earlier section of this chapter. Do well to refer to that section when you feel that keeping your soulmate in the loop is unnecessary.

While it feels great to be in a relationship with your soulmate, you must know that it will not work without effort. If your love will go the way you want and lead to a happy ending, you must be willing to give it your best shot. Pay attention to the tips discussed in this chapter and watch your love stay secure and grow.

If you enjoyed this chapter about how to make love work in your relationship, I just know you're going to love the next chapter about how sex plays a role in keeping your soulmate.

See you in the next chapter!

CHAPTER 7: HOW SEX PLAYS A ROLE IN KEEPING YOUR SOULMATE

Ignore sex at your own peril

SEX; one of the most controversial and misunderstood words in relationships. Many feelings are elicited in many people's minds at the mention of this word. For some people, sex is that thing that should not be talked about, heard about, or even thought of until one is married.

These people believe that parents should not even have the *"sex"* conversation with their adolescent children because they would be corrupting them or feeding them the wrong information.

For the people in this category, if someone thinks of sex without being in a marriage, they believe that person has some sort of moral challenge.

Sitting pretty at the other side of the pendulum are people who believe that *"sex"* is terrific. From the time these people hit adolescence and figured out what their sexual organs were for, they began a never-ending journey of exploration; chasing down sexual fantasies and living in the moment.

For people in this category, life is nothing without a bit of fun and the thrill of intense pleasure that comes with having sexual contact with another person. When they eventually get into a romantic relationship, they quickly assess their partner's sexual prowess. If their partner is not up to par, they may have to call the relationship quits.

When it comes to sex, you must understand that it is a significant part of any relationship. Especially if you want your relationship to last for a long time and lead to a *'happily-ever-after.'* This is because of the significance of sex and the bond it creates in people's lives in a relationship.

In any case, we will look at the subject of *"sex"* and evaluate the role it must play in your relationship with your soulmate if you want a relationship that never ends.

What is 'SEX?'

It seems like a silly question to ask. When we talk about 'sex,' we're not referring to the gender you were born as or the one you identify with at the moment. Sex in this context is the verb, the physical act of joining as one with your soulmate.

Wikipedia defines *'sex'* with the phrase; *"human sexual activity/human sexual practice."*

According to Wikipedia, this is how humans express and experience a spiritual awakening. *"Spiritual"* not in the religious sense, but in a total *"out-of-body"* experience, almost like a drug high.

As a matter of fact, sex is a broad term that encompasses a multitude of actions aimed at giving those involved in the act *(yourself and your soulmate, in this context)* an avenue to express themselves and experience the feelings, passion, attraction, and lust of the other person.

This action dates back to the beginning of time, and the need to have physical contact with another person is a thirst that everyone is bound to experience in their lives at some point.

What you need to know about sex

Before we get on with the subject, there are some records we must set straight. These are the mainstream ideas that may hold you back and prevent you from having a fulfilling sexual experience, even when you are with your soulmate. Please note these points that I discuss in this section before proceeding and completing this chapter.

1. **It is difficult to define the right/wrong way to have sex**

This is one thing you need to know about the subject of sex; there is no one-size-fits-all approach to it. Although this may sound a bit far-fetched to you, there are different strokes for different folks in this context, literally.

If you must have a satisfying sexual life with your soulmate, you must understand that some of the things that make you tick will not set off their alarms at all. There are about a thousand different sexual activities, and you may discover that your soulmate has a preference for sexual activity you may not have heard of before.

What this also implies is that you may not be abnormal as you may think you are. Many people are held back from exploring the boundaries of their sexual lives with their soulmates simply because they have sexual urges that they believe are unhealthy or unheard of. This may not be true.

Since it is difficult to define a right/wrong approach to sex, you must consciously set a boundary to it. As is the case with every healthy thing, you must understand what you accept or otherwise do not. While doing this, pay attention and make sure that what you believe is fun for you does not hurt the other person involved.

Sex is about pleasure and an avenue to express your love for your soulmate. It should not be used as an outlet or a way to inflict pain on your partner or, vice versa, to deal with stress in your life.

2. To enjoy sex, you must be comfortable

This is one thing that not many people today possess: comfort. In today's world, comfort looks like a far-fetched topic. Here is what is meant by comfort.

Comfort, in this context, is the feeling of satisfaction that comes from knowing that you are human and unforgettable just the way you are. Although many people today walk around in the best of clothes and look satisfied with themselves, a good number of them are not comfortable. This discomfort is the result of several reasons, including:

A. Unhealthy comparisons

This is usually the result of an internalized action, generally known as *"body shaming."* Body Shaming is the practice of making a mockery of someone by criticizing or making them feel horrible about their body size or shape. Body shaming can be internal *(happening within the person)* or external *(coming from other people)*.

When people are compared or compare themselves against others like the picture-perfect models they see in movies or music videos or just someone they would rather look like, the result is that over time, they begin to look down on their bodies. Under these conditions, they start believing that they are not attractive. Any compliment about their body shape will be taken as a form of criticism.

A person who struggles with body-shaming is not likely to enjoy sex with their partner. Because they are already cynical toward themselves, they are unwilling to take compliments *(even in the heat of the physical activity)*. They will most likely not loosen up enough to enjoy intimacy with their partner.

B. The idea that they are 'weird'

When someone harbors the notion that they are weird or strange for some reason (especially regarding their sexuality and sexual preferences), there is every tendency that they will be unable to loosen up enough and enjoy sex with their partner.

Sometimes, this idea of weirdness comes when the person discovers that they like something that is not mainstream, that they have some strange fetish, and they may not know that there exist other people just like themselves.

The way around this is to start by exposing yourself to the world. Take some time to get out of your head. To achieve this, you may want to talk to an expert on sexual health or a psychologist who can help you break down what you feel and show you how you may want to go about it to get the best results.

3. An active sex life can prove to be a vital part of your relationship

While this may be a subjective statement, it still holds true. Some people may not agree that sex is vital except when married to your soulmate.

Others may see sex as a non-negotiable factor in the relationship. In any case, sex is essential, and that is what we will spend the rest of this chapter discusses.

For the best results, you may want to spend some time talking to your soulmate about what they believe and hold as true when it comes to sex. This is the only way to make sure that both of you are on the same page regarding sex.

4. For sex to work, you must be compatible with your partner

This is related to the first point I made in this section of the program; different people have different sexual preferences.

Pay attention to your partner and be sure to understand their sexual preferences. This way, you can know what they want and how you can meet their sexual needs.

Why do people have sex?

Now that we have cleared the air and established a few things you need to know about sex, we must examine why people have sex. When we have explained these, you will begin to understand why you feel the urge to have sex with your soulmate *(or maybe not)*.

1.   Sex is an expression of deep emotions

As hinted in the definition of sex, one of the primary reasons people have sex is that sex is a channel through which they can express their feelings to their soulmate, especially when they want this to go beyond words.

This goes beyond the mindless activity of having a quick romp in the sack with another random person.

Under these conditions *(when they want to express their feelings for their soulmate)*, they refer to it as *"making love."*

This phrase implies that they are doing more than the physical activity. To them, it is about the emotional and psychological connection that accompanies having sex *(or making love)*.

2.   To achieve a desired aim

Although this may sound obvious, many people have sex to achieve a desired aim. When the objective is met, there is little or no commitment from either party. Some of these goals may include having a baby, improve a person's social standing *(move from low status in a group to become much more popular)*, or exerting revenge in some cases.

3. Pressure

This is the side of sex that is not pleasing at all. Sometimes, people have sex because of the pressure they come under.

This pressure could be from friends *(to conquer the fear of missing out or feel like they belong)* or the pressure from a partner *(which they may give in to so that they can stop being pestered or as a way of preventing something terrible from happening like the exit of that partner from a relationship)*.

Notwithstanding what form it takes, having sex because of being placed under undue pressure is not healthy for you. As much as it lies within you, walk away from any person or situation where you are pressured to have sex, especially when you feel like you are not yet ready for it.

4. Sexual curiosity

Some people do not begin their sexual journey with the assuredness of who they really are or what they want sexually from their partner. This leads to confusion when they meet someone that they feel attraction for.

These people are usually curious and have many things on their minds.

As a result of the confusion they experience, they may begin to try out many things sexually. This confusion leads to their having sex because of curiosity. Sometimes, they may find the answers they seek. Sometimes, they may not.

Why is sex important in maintaining relationships?

Let's deep-dive into several reasons why sex is essential in relationships.

1. **The emotional connection that comes with it**

In the previous section, we established that sex is important because it provides people with a channel to express their emotions. This is one of the first reasons why sex is essential in your relationship with your soulmate.

If you are looking to transform the words "I love you" to a new form of expression where your soulmate begins to trust and believe it for real, you may want to try adding sex to your relationship.

Under these conditions, you must not approach sex as an activity you are compelled to engage in. Instead, you must work hard to make it a memorable experience for your partner and make sure that you can communicate your emotions' depths with them.

2. **A healthy sex life can help you/your partner build self-esteem**

Remember how we discussed body shaming and how it can threaten a person's sexual life? A healthy sex life with your partner can serve to help you regain your self-esteem *(if you have lost it at some point)* or vice versa *(if your partner is the one affected)*.

During the act, your partner's love, attention, and adoration are channeled toward you while you do the same thing for them. Being in the center, love and attention can be pivotal toward helping you regain your sense of self-esteem.

As your partner tells you how beautiful you are to them, these words and reassurance can override the effects of every bad word and thought you might have harbored about yourself in years past.

As you allow this action to go on and continue over time, your partner's assertions and emotions start getting registered in your subconscious, and this is what accounts for the surge in self-esteem that you will notice.

For this to work, your partner needs to be lavish with attention and care even while they make love to you. If your partner also needs a self-esteem boost, you must be conscious about returning the favor.

3. The reproductive factor

This is one of the foremost reasons why people have sex; for the sake of reproduction. If you are married to your soulmate, or you are not opposed to the idea of having children, you may want to get physically involved with your partner so that the both of you can make children while at it.

4. Stress relief

Research shows that sex is a great way to eliminate stress and tension when these weigh down on you. This is yet another reason why sex must be a part of your relationship with your soulmate.

If you are the kind that gets stressed all the time *(or your partner is)*, there is every tendency that they would love to relate to you sexually. Allowing yourself to get involved in the act can afford you the opportunity to help your soulmate get rid of stress while they return the favor to you as well.

5. Health benefits

Surprisingly, there are many health benefits associated with a healthy sex life. Some of them include:

A. *Sex can be a mild form of exercise.*

This should not be shocking because there is a reason why you work up a sweat when you have had sex. A survey carried out corroborated this theory. So, you may want to add that to the pool of reasons why you would incorporate sex into your list of activities to be done with your soulmate.

B. People with a healthy sex life are generally healthier than those who do not have this.

The immune systems of people with a good sex life seem to perform better, and they are known to be stronger, maintaining a healthy balance in life. They get sick less often and recover from illness faster.

C. Improved memory.

A study was carried out which showed that people between the ages of 50-90, who have a healthy sex life, are more likely to have better memories than their age mates who do not have positive sex lives.

When all these health benefits are looked at, you can safely say that with healthy sex in your relationship, there are more reasons for you and your partner to enjoy the relationship and stay together longer, if not forever.

6. **A healthy sex life strengthens your relationship beyond the four walls of your bedroom**

When it comes to your sex life, the rewards you get when you have a healthy one goes beyond the four walls of your bedroom. It is easy to identify people who have been intimate with each other, even when you see them outside the bedroom. For these people, there is an affection and ease that they feel around one another.

If your love language is personal touch, you may find the ease that comes with being intimate with your soulmate as an incentive for them to be cozy with you and not ashamed to express their love for you even in public.

However, for the sake of decency, you may want to keep things appropriate for all audiences when you are in public.

7.   After great sex comes a good night's sleep

If you or your partner battles insomnia, you may want to pay more attention to this point. Research and patterns have shown that after great sex, the body's natural response falls into a state of deep sleep. So, here's how it works:

At the climax of sexual activity, your body releases an enzyme known as Prolactin. Among many things that "prolactin" does, it can lead to deeper and more relaxed sleep and more intriguing dreams *(better sleep in the REM phase)*.

This is why once you orgasm; your body's next response is to fall into a state of satisfaction, and if you aren't careful to prevent it from happening, you will discover that your eyes will begin to slip shut.

How to be a better lover for your lover

It is not enough to understand what sex is and why it is vital in your relationship. You must know how to make yourself a better lover for your soulmate.

That was the whole idea behind this chapter; to equip you with the knowledge you need to become a better lover. To become better with your lover, here are a few things you must do:

1. **Normalize being vulnerable with them**

This is one of the basic requirements for having sex with your soulmate. If you are to enjoy the activity, you must allow yourself to become vulnerable with them and let go of control at some point. Sex is all about trust, and to trust someone, you must allow yourself to become vulnerable.

2. **Listen to them as well**

We are talking about a relationship here, not a one-sided case of infatuation and misguided emotions. To make the most of your sexual life with your soulmate/partner, understand that it is not all about you.

They have needs just like you do, and listening to them not only makes them feel appreciated, but it also instructs you to know what you must do to make your sex life better.

3. Be intentional about showing your soulmate love and respect as you make love to them

Especially if you know that they either suffer from body shaming or battle with low self-esteem. The psychology behind this has been explained in-depth in earlier sections of this chapter.

Be sure to add this to your bucket list of activities because once your partner builds their self-esteem, it will show during sex. They may have the audacity to try out new stuff with you, thereby spicing up your sex life.

4. Teach yourself to speak their love language

Above and beyond the physical activity, you seek an experience with your soulmate. An experience of intimacy and oneness with them. To achieve this, you need much more than sex. You must know how to make your partner feel loved and appreciated when they are with you.

One way to do this is by teaching yourself how to speak your partners' love language. When you begin to express their love language, you will notice that they get more attuned to you like a blooming flower.

As this happens, rest assured that you are getting them to trust you, and this will make the lovemaking experience with them much better as time moves forward.

How to get your lover to be better for you

Just as we established earlier, it is a two-way street. Apply the following strategies to get your lover to be a better lover for you:

1. **Talk to them**

Your soulmate is not some ghost with superpowers of knowing everything. Do not assume that your soulmate knows what you like and what you do not with respect to your sexual life and preferences. It is your duty to educate them and do this as many times as needed.

2. **Be ready to compromise**

Since you are striving to build an enviable future with your soulmate, one way to win this war can be to put down your verbal-gun at some point and decide to call a truce.

In this context, this means connecting with your soulmate *(by practicing step one above)* and deciding on how to do things so that everyone benefits in the end.

They may not be able to meet all of your sexual needs, but the idea is that they get to a point where they meet most of your needs.

Healthy compromise is one way to do this. Sex is a significant part of most healthy relationships. If you chose to allow it to be a part of your relationship, it is imperative that you do it properly by using the tips and strategies discussed in this chapter.

As you just learned, sex can play a positive role in your relationship, but finding your soulmate does not guarantee that your relationship will last forever. In the next chapter, I explain to you why.

See you in the next chapter!

CHAPTER 8: WHY FINDING YOUR SOULMATE DOES NOT GUARANTEE THE RELATIONSHIP WILL LAST LONG

Nothing in life is guaranteed, especially love!

You may have harbored ideas peddled by romance movies and sappy books. These ideas usually show that once soulmates have found themselves, they fight through many challenges and stroll into a happily-ever-after.

While this happens at times, you must face reality here; and the truth is that this is not always the case. Even after meeting your soulmate, there is no guarantee that you will be together for the rest of your lives. For one, they may be married or tethered to someone else (and happily so).

They may not be seeking anything more from you than friendship, or something else may stop you from getting the happy ending you desire with your soulmate.

In any case, things may not work out, even after you have found your soulmate. This chapter will examine this uncommon truth and see why this happens to some people and steps you can take to reduce it from happening to you.

So you think that you have found your soulmate?

This program's whole point is to open your eyes to what you must do to find your soulmate and offer guidance on what you must do when you have found them.

However, you may be at a point where you try to make things work with a person you believe is your soulmate. If you take a step back and discover that you are doing your best to make things work with them and things are not, you may want to ask yourself a critical question. Are they indeed the one?

Asking and answering this question can be instrumental as it will open your eyes to see if you are walking the right path or wasting your time and resources on a person you should not be.

No matter how far you think you have traveled down the relationship road, you must look out for red flags that show you are with the wrong person.

You cannot make things work with the wrong

person, no matter how hard you try. Here are a few red flags; signs that the person you think is your soulmate is not who you think they are.

1.   You both want different things

Remember how we discussed that with your soulmate, you should know that you both want the same things? This is not the case with a person who is not your soulmate. Even if you look at them and feel the chemistry, this is one factor you must consider carefully before committing to anything with anyone.

Your *"non-soulmate"* will be on a different journey, and most times, you will discover that what you want and what they want are two opposite ends that should never meet.

In line with this, your values will be different, and your attitude towards life will be dissimilar. Priorities will not be complementary, and in general, the both of you will be like the North and South poles *(too distant to interact with yourselves).*

The result of this is that your relationship will be fraught with differences, and challenges will keep coming up as you go. A clear example is that you may want to have a large family while they may not want kids at all. This one thing can create a massive gap between the both of you and drive the relationship into the ground.

2. They won't return your gesture of honesty and openness

Honesty is a critical part of every successful relationship, and although you will be interested in making things work, they will not be too eager to return the gesture.

You will discover that there is a lot of secrecy and hiding with this person. They will be more likely to trust other people, except you, and find it hard to have conversations where they will need to be vulnerable with you.

3. They will give you hints

We often get hints that a person should not be there in our lives. They may not say it with their mouths, but their actions and everything in between will tell you that they are not the one for you.

You will notice that all your love and attention is one-sided, and when you try to confront them, they may come clean with you and tell you that you are not the one for them.

As much as this pulling away may be one of the most challenging things for you to do, your best line of action will be to pull the plug on the relationship. Walk away because you deserve better.

4. **They abuse you**

Abusing you is one red flag you cannot afford to turn blind eyes to. Your soulmate understands the value of your sanity and will do nothing to compromise it. On the other hand, when you are with someone who is not your soulmate and who has little or no affection for you, they do not see abusing you as a big deal.

Abuse comes in many forms, and you do not have to wait until the person hits you or does anything to harm your body for you to see the signs before you. The wrong person may subject you to other forms of abuse that are not physical but mental and emotional in nature.

They do this to exercise control over you and get you under their grip. This is the bottom line of abuse, and making excuses for them will not change the fact that you need to confront the facts before you immediately.

5. **They aren't there for you**

There are times when you need the attention of your soulmate, but they may be unable to rise to the occasion. This can be understandable and utterly different from what we discuss in this section.

The wrong person is never there for you when you need them. Usually, this happens more than once. Since both of you will most likely have different interests, there is every tendency that they will never be able to support you.

For any relationship to work, support is crucial, and this must come from both sides of the relationship. When your partner makes it a point of duty to let you handle everything in your life all by yourself *(physically, mentally, emotionally, and in every dimension)*, this may be a sign that you are with the wrong person.

6. **They talk down on your vision**

Your soulmate should be your biggest cheerleader. However, when you discover that the person you want to make things work with is continuously in the business of making you feel stupid for having big dreams, take that as a sign of something more serious.

As a result, your self-esteem may be harmed. You may get to a point where it feels as though you cannot achieve a lot, and you may lose the zeal to be optimistic about life while still pursuing your ambitions. Being with the wrong person does more to you than just physically hurting you.

Why soulmate relationships do not always work out

As much as this may not be the most effortless conversation for you, finding your soulmate is not always a guarantee that the relationship will work out.

If the person you are with does not tick the points communicated in the last section, you want to consider the next few issues. These are reasons why soulmates do not always end up together.

1. **When you meet your soulmate at the wrong time of life**

In an earlier chapter, we explored the concept of the wrong time in detail. The truth is, if you meet your soulmate at this time, you will have to fight through a lot to make things work. However, if they are not interested in fighting for you as well, the relationship may not blossom.

For example, suppose you meet your soulmate and discover that they are happily married to someone else and are in no way looking to get out of the marriage. In that case, there is every tendency that your relationship with them will not lead to a happily-ever-after.

Another classic example of this is if you meet your soulmate at a time when they are straight out of a bad relationship, still hurting deeply, and in no place to look for anything more. Your relationship with them will be negatively affected.

2. **Demands from society and loved ones**

Although this sounds like something from the 1800s, some parents still forbid their children from marrying or dating someone of a different racial or ethnic background. This can prove challenging as you look to build a life with your soulmate after finding them.

Although they may love you, this person may feel a deep sense of indebtedness to their parents and may not want to go against them.

Religion can pose a substantial barrier to being with your soulmate. Some religions believe and teach that it is a sin and wrong for a person who is part of them to marry someone from another religious background.

This forms a significant block when building a life with your soulmate. Although they might love you, they need the blessings and approval of their family and religious leader to pursue a long-term commitment with you.

There is also the challenge of societal views on specific subjects. The issue of a person's sexuality and gender identification can threaten you if you are looking to build a life with them. For example, if a man found out that his soulmate is of the same gender, pursuing a relationship with him may be challenging or downright impossible *(depending on the societal context in question)*.

The result is that many people have been pushed to the point where they have to let go of their soulmate or began to live lives of secrecy while still living up to the demands that society, family, or religious groups have placed on them.

3. **Personal challenges**

Some soulmate relationships end up not

blossoming because one or both partners may be dealing with acute personal problems. One partner may not be inclined towards being on the receiving end of such issues for long.

For example, it's not easy to deal with a soulmate that overanalyzes everything *(every gesture and conversation)*, is cynical and does not trust you. This alone can be a dealbreaker on different levels.

4. Unrealistic expectations

If you do not make it a point of duty to correct this immediately, you may fall into this trap. Your soulmate is a person that is meant for you. You feel a deep connection between both of you, and sometimes this may even be on a spiritual level. This does not negate the fact that your soulmate is human and that there is only so much they can do for you.

Unrealistic expectations can kill your relationship and make a quick mess of it; that is if you let it consume you. Yes, there are things your soulmate must-do for you. Do not make it a point of duty to believe that they will be there for you at every turn.

Unrealistic expectations, like the belief that your soulmate relationship will be nothing short of beautiful, will only cause you untold heartache. If not careful, you might throw this relationship away simply because you got your hopes too far up in the sky.

Your soulmate is human and having unrealistic expectations will place them under undue pressure. As time proceeds, this can cause your relationship to fail.

5. **People change**

This is one thing you must know if you will be successful with your relationship. Although they may be the one for you presently, people change in the future. You and your partner may become very different people 2, 5 or even 20 years from today.

At the beginning of your journey, they may want you; craving your love, attention, and all that. However, you may notice a few drastic changes as time unfolds. The passage of time may reveal that they are changing, just like everything in life does. Many people ask the million-dollar question: *"Why has my partner changed?"* To proceed, we must answer this question in-depth.

Here are a few reasons why people change.

A. Growth

Personal growth is a significant and foundational reason why people change. When you grow, you discover a different approach to life, a new set of values, new priorities, and many things about you become new.

Take this as an example: When you were a child, some games were the highlight of your life. You lived for them, looked forward to them, and spent your free time playing these games.

When you became a teenager, these games changed meaning for you. As you grew into adulthood, you shed them entirely and moved on to grapple with the challenges of adulthood. It happens the same way with your soulmate.

When they begin to grow *(in age and other dimensions of life)*, there is every tendency that you will notice new things about them. They may stop being the people you knew, adopt new lifestyles, and these may affect your relationship; either positively or negatively.

Growth will change your soulmate in more ways than you expected, especially as they begin to grapple with more responsibilities.

B. Exposure that increases options

Exposure is an important point we must discuss in this chapter. *Exposure (or options)* comes with a change in the way people see things and how they interact with life. Exposure widens a person's options.

Consider this scenario: You met your soulmate as a college student. Both of you happen to be college classmates. It is love at first sight, and you can almost vow that you will be together forever.

That is great until both of you are done with college and you move to different parts of the country to get established and seek opportunities that can help you become all you want in life. In the new place, you meet a new person, and they catch your fancy in ways you never expected.

You feel connected with this new person, although you promised yourself you would not. As much as you try to turn blind eyes to it, you cannot rule out the fact that there is something about this new person that draws you in. What do you think will happen when after a period of being with this new person?

Do you think that you will have the same enthusiasm to see your sweetheart from college again? Do you think things will automatically revert to the way they were before?

One thing happened to you - exposure. Your options increased, and you started questioning what you knew before. This can happen to your soulmate when exposed to more options.

Exposure is a significant factor responsible for drastic changes in people. They may have met someone else and now believe that you are not their soulmate after all. The way to make sure that you are not making a mistake is by giving yourself more options.

Even when you have found the one you believe is your soulmate, you may want to take some time to explore more options before making a lasting commitment. Meet more people, travel, and have fun. The same applies to your soulmate.

C. People get bored

At the beginning of your relationship, you were excited. The novelty of all that you felt for them excited you in no small way. The same could be said for them until this relationship started getting older.

Suddenly, your soulmate began to change how they relate to you. This may result from getting tired of the relationship or the lack of thrill in it.

Humans are excitement freaks. We enjoy the thrill of something new. That is why it is easier to start a new business than to grow an existing one. When your soulmate gets tired of the relationship, they may begin to act flippant, dismissive of you, eager to spend more time away from you. They may get apathetic toward everything that has to do with the relationship.

At this point, the spark dies down. The chemistry you felt at the beginning can almost be thought of as a thing of the past. To salvage the relationship, you need to seek ways to bring back the relationship's spice. All your activities at this point should point toward rekindling the flame of your passion - the one you felt at the beginning.

If you do not do this, you run the risk of losing your soulmate to the next available person as your partner searches for excitement.

How can these changes affect your relationship, and what you can do about them

Changes in attitude and character can affect your relationship in many ways. Some of them include:

1. Your partner begins to see you in ways they did not before.

In this context, this is a bad way. You no longer look sexy enough for them, and their interest in continuing the relationship drops. You may want to spend some time talking with them.

This is one case where complete honesty and openness are needed in a relationship. Listen to them and hear what it is about you that they are less excited about and the things they would rather that you start doing. With this knowledge, you can tweak things and improve your relationship.

2. When the trigger for this change is

exposure (other options), you will notice that someone else becomes the center of your partner's world.

They would rather spend more time with that person than with you. They may start keeping secrets and acting suspiciously when you are around.

If your partner got exposed to someone else and decide that this new person is better for them after all, it is best to grant them their wish. Take a bow and let them go. This will not be easy; especially if you have come to love and cherish them. Realize that you have options too. In a previous chapter, I gave you many ways to meet your soulmate. You may need to dust off that chapter and use it again.

You should never need to beg anyone to be with you. Your true soulmate will want you as much as you want them.

Signs that you are not your partner's soulmate

Is it possible to feel a soulmate connection with someone who does not feel the same way for you? One-sided affections are everywhere in life. Here are signs that you are not your partner's soulmate. These points should help you start putting things into perspective.

1. When you are not your partner's soulmate, you end up giving more than you receive.

This implies that you are the one who makes all the moves and acts as though the relationship is essential. They stand back and soak in all the attention while behaving as though they are entitled to the love and attention you shower on them.

2. They have qualities that are a no-nos for you, and they are not willing to work on these; even for you.

In their opinion, you have got to love them the way they are, but they do not hesitate to let you know the things they want you to do and the ways they want you to change for them. And yes, they expect you to do exactly as they say but never return the favor.

3. They feel uncomfortable around you, which continues even as the relationship keeps unfolding.

This discomfort is evident in how they relate with you and their unlikeliness to confide in you or trust what you say to them.

4. They are never satisfied with anything you do.

You are never good enough. You always must try harder; do more to earn their approval and attention; and fit into a predefined character for them to be proud of you. If they could, they would shed you in a heartbeat.

When you notice these points in a relationship, these are indicators that you are not with your soulmate, no matter how strongly you feel about them. The best line of action may be to take a step back.

As much as it is a bitter pill to swallow, soulmate relationships do not always lead to marriage or long-term commitments.

This chapter has been dedicated to opening you up to red flags to look out for when relating to your soulmate. Signs that you are not with your soulmate, and what to do if you discover that your partner is not your soulmate.

I also introduced you to the concept of *change* and showed you what you must do when you notice changes in your partner *(negative changes)*. Make use of this information as you define your relationship's next steps.

Once you internalize that finding your soulmate is no guarantee of success, you can start looking at love realistically and mentally prepare yourself should it fail.

In the final chapter, I want to wrap up all that you've learned about finding your soulmate. You can start to put the action steps in this program into motion this weekend.

See you in the next chapter!

CONCLUSION

Your desire to find and build a stable relationship with your soulmate is commendable. If there is one thing you should know by now; IT IS POSSIBLE.

You may have suffered through a lot in the past. You may have gone through terrible relationships *(or at least relationships that you were not proud of)*. You may have had people laugh at you and tell you that there is no such thing as a *'soulmate,'* but you know better. You will soon prove them wrong.

Your special person is out there, somewhere. And it is your job to position yourself as the kind of person they would want to be with. You must prove to the Universe that you are ready for the blessing of finding and being with your soulmate. Prepare to fight for them and your relationship when you finally meet them.

This program has been a guide to help you through all these steps. And so that these steps remain fresh in your mind, here's a quick recap of the major lessons you have learned in the preceding pages of this blueprint.

1. **You must start your journey to finding your soulmate and true love from a place of finding yourself.**

   You cannot give what you do not have. It will be impossible for you to love your soulmate *(when you finally meet them)* if you have issues loving and accepting yourself. Loving yourself completely is a conscious action and one you must execute before you set out to find your soulmate.

2. **You must let go of the past and become vulnerable.**

   You will not succeed in your quest to find and build forever with your soulmate if you hang on to the mistakes, hurt, and bitterness from the past. Take the past as an incentive to live an ideal present. Reach into the future you deserve; a future of love and happiness with your soulmate.

3. **The Universe is waiting for you and is willing to bring your soulmate your way.**

   This knowledge will help cement in you the consciousness that there is someone out there for you. If you do all you should *(follow through with all the steps discussed in different chapters of this* program*),* your soulmate will come to you.

4. **To find your soulmate, you must be actively involved in the process.**

    Although the Universe is willing to help you, you must understand that this connection with your soulmate is ultimately the result of a collaborative effort.

    You must be willing to do your part and put in the work discussed in the beginning chapters of this program while still holding on to the faith that your soulmate will find you.

5. **Timing is everything in this quest to find your soulmate.**

    It is possible to find your soulmate at the wrong time. If this ever happens to you, the journey to getting together and building a meaningful relationship with them will be difficult *(if not downright impossible).*

    However, you can do a few things to make sure that timing works in your favor. These were discussed in-depth in the 4th chapter of this program.

6. **Your soulmate may not come into your life the way you expect.**

   You may think of your soulmate as royalty who will step into your life to save the day when you are in a dire situation. You may think of them as the holy divine one who will move into the home just across yours this summer.

   While these may end up happening for you, it is not always the case. Your soulmate will often come on the scene in the most unconventional ways.

   There is every chance that you have met them already, but because you did not know what to look for, this person slipped away from you into the arms of someone else.

   Therefore, you must know the signs that show that your soulmate has come into your life. These signs were explained in-depth in the 5th chapter.

7. **A beautiful relationship with your soulmate will have its prickly thorns.**

   Your soulmate is human *(just as you are)*, and to make your relationship work with them, you must commit to it. Challenges will come as the days and months unfold. There will be times when you may be tempted to call it quits and go your separate ways. However, you must learn to make your love work for you.

This is what the 6th chapter of this program taught in detail. Love and your relationship with your soulmate are no walks in the park. Equip yourself with the tips discussed in chapter 6 as you journey to the future you desire.

8. **Do not trivialize the subject of physical intimacy with your partner.**

    This applies to you more if your partner believes that expressing feelings and establishing a deep connection in a relationship requires sexual contact.

    Sex is vital, and at the start of your relationship, you may want to have this conversation with your partner.

    Please pay attention to what they say, what they do not say, and commit to spicing up your relationship in line with the compromise you reach between yourselves. Chapter 7 discussed the subject of 'sex' and how it affects your relationship with your soulmate.

9. **Change is constant, and we discussed the concept of change in terms of your relationship with your soulmate in chapter 8.**

At the beginning of your journey, you dreamed of a loving, attentive partner who enjoys your company. The day you find this person, it feels incredible and somewhat intoxicating.

But have you stopped to think of what will happen if, suddenly, your partner begins to change for the worst? How do you handle the nagging thoughts that keep telling you that your bliss will be short-lived?

How do you ensure that you will build forever with your soulmate and that this relationship will not end up as another conquest you will have to move on from tomorrow?

Nothing is guaranteed in life; not even your relationship with your soulmate. Equip yourself with the strategies for handling changes in yourself and your partner, which was discussed in the last chapter of this program.

My earnest desire is to see you break free from the shackles holding you back from positioning yourself for love. I want that you meet the person of your dreams *(your soulmate)* and build an enviable, long-term relationship with them.

That is why I made this program practical and full of life lessons to apply in your relationship with your soulmate today. Go through this program many times *(so the messages can register in your subconscious)* and begin to work on all action points extracted from these pages.

Above all, believe that you can, and you should - FIND LOVE IN YOUR SOULMATE. Then reach out to the relationship of a lifetime. You deserve the most profound love of your soulmate.

Grab Your FREE Gift on the Next Page

YOUR FREE GIFT

Finding Your Soulmate Tips Sheet

Sometimes you need a quick tip for a situation.
This tips sheet points you to the best resources
to help you fast!
(Get Yours Now...It's FREE)

Request FREE Tips Sheet Today. Go to:
https://loveblueprints.com/soulmate-tips-sheet/

Reference List

Booth, H. (2019, May 20). *"Start low and go slow": how to talk to your partner about sex.* The Guardian. https://www.theguardian.com/lifeandstyle/2019/may/20/start-low-and-go-slow-how-to-talk-to-your-partner-about-sex

Center, R. T. (2019, August 11). *True Love vs. Infatuation.* Restorations Therapy Center. https://www.restorationstherapy.com/true-love-vs-infatuation/

Development, R. (2019, December 1). *Don't date girls who have lots of male friends.* Rebellious Development. https://rebelliousdevelopment.com/dont-date-girls-who-have-male-friends/

Donovan, L. (2014, February 20). *10 Places You Could Meet Your Future Soulmate.*

HelloGiggles.
https://hellogiggles.com/lifestyle/10-places-meet-future-soulmate/

Fellizar, K. (2018, October 1). *7 Signs You're Not Actually Your Partner's Soulmate, You're Just Their Type*. Bustle.
https://www.bustle.com/p/7-signs-youre-not-actually-your-partners-soulmate-youre-just-their-type-12108991

Gustafson, D. A. L. (2014, May 4). *8 Ways to Grow Love*. HuffPost.
https://www.huffpost.com/entry/eight-ways-to-grow-love_b_4894123

Harra, C., & Harra, A. (2016, May 5). *7 Qualities To Seek In A Soulmate*. HuffPost.
https://www.huffpost.com/entry/7-qualities-to-seek-in-a-_b_7201494

Kassel, G. (2020, January 24). *6 Reasons Why Sex Is Important in a Relationship*. Well+Good.

https://www.wellandgood.com/why-is-sex-important-relationship/

Kirschner, D. (2020, January 14). *When You Find Your Soulmate at the Wrong Time*. Love in 90 Days. https://lovein90days.com/when-you-find-your-soulmate-at-the-wrong-time/

Laderer, A. (2019, October 18). *How Your Partner's Past Might Impact Your Future*. Talkspace. https://www.talkspace.com/blog/partners-past-impact-your-future/

Laura, V. A. P. B. V. (2019, November 27). *5 Places Where you could Meet your Soulmate*. WordPress.Com. https://valentinalaura.com/2017/08/19/5-places-where-you-could-meet-your-soulmate/

Lawrence, S. (2019, June 10). *3 Signs That You Have Instant Chemistry Because You Loved Each Other In A Past Life*. YourTango. https://www.yourtango.com/experts/sarah-lawrence/how-to-tell-if-you-have-found-love-

with-your-soulmate-or-if-its-a-karmic-
relationship-from-your-past-life

Leasca, S. (2020, August 24). *13 Best Online Dating
Sites to Find Love in 2020*. Glamour.
https://www.glamour.com/story/best-online-
dating-sites-to-find-love

Leonie, C. (2020, March 9). *Why Some Soulmate
Relationships Don't Last*. Caren Reads.
https://www.carenreads.com/question-of-the-
week-why-some-soulmate-relationships-dont-
last-forever/

M. (2020, September 19). *When You Meet Your
Soulmate At The Wrong Time*. Thought
Catalog. https://thoughtcatalog.com/marissa-
hernandez/2015/02/when-you-meet-your-
soulmate-at-the-wrong-time/

Mellardo, A. (2017, March 9). *How To Tell If He's
Confident, Or Cocky*. Elite Daily.
https://www.elitedaily.com/dating/ways-tell-
guy-dating-confident-cocky/1819258

Ohlin, B. (2020, November 7). *7 Ways to Improve Communication in Relationships*. PositivePsychology.Com. https://positivepsychology.com/communication-in-relationships/

Positivity, P. O. (2019, May 1). *How to Tell If Your Partner Is Your Soulmate (Or Not)*. Power of Positivity: Positive Thinking & Attitude. https://www.powerofpositivity.com/partner-doesnt-11-qualities-theyre-not-soulmate/

Pugachevsky, J. (2018, May 16). *7 Types Of Bad Men And Why You Keep Dating Them*. Cosmopolitan. https://www.cosmopolitan.com/sex-love/a20159874/how-to-stop-dating-bad-people/

Reid, S. (2016, October 14). *15 Reasons Why You Shouldn't Date A Mama's Boy*. TheTalko. https://www.thetalko.com/15-reasons-why-you-shouldnt-date-a-mamas-boy/

Santoro. (2013, June 30). *Are You Prepared for Love? 5 Ways to Prepare Yourself!* HuffPost. https://www.huffpost.com/entry/finding-love_b_3179023

Schreiber, K. (2016, January 14). *Yes, Being Vulnerable Is Terrifying—But Here's Why It's So Worth It*. Greatist. https://greatist.com/live/fear-of-vulnerability

T. (2018, April 15). *When Soulmates Meet At The Wrong Time - TheLoveWitchProject*. Medium. https://medium.com/@thelovewitchpro/when-soulmates-meet-at-the-wrong-time-2602cb8d19fc

Therapist, T. A. (2018, June 13). *Do you know your love language? (and why it's important)*. Medium. https://angrytherapist.medium.com/do-you-know-your-love-language-and-why-its-important-35c36ab986cc

Understanding Past Relationships. (2020, May 17). Therapy In Philadelphia. https://www.therapyinphiladelphia.com/tips/understanding-past-relationships

Weiss, J. (2017, January 21). *How to Use Your Intuition To Attract Your Soul Mate*. JIM WEISS. https://www.jimweiss.net/use-your-intuition-to-attract-your-soul-mate/

Long Distance Love

The Blueprint to Starting a Long-Distance Relationship that is Fun and Successful.

By Christopher Conway

YOUR FREE GIFT

Long Distance Love Tips Sheet

Sometimes you need a quick tip for a situation. This tips sheet points you to the best resources to help you fast!
(Get Yours Now...It's FREE)

Request FREE Tips Sheet Today. Go to:
https://LoveBlueprints.com/love-tips-sheet/

INTRODUCTION

You did it. You found the one person that makes your heart pound when you speak to them. You spend the early hours of every morning thinking about them. The mere thought of them sends goosebumps up and down the spine of your back. You wish you could spend every waking minute next to them. There is a catch, though.

The catch is that this person lives in another city, state, or even a different country. How can you make this relationship last forever? How will you hold this relationship together long enough until you are finally together in the same city? Hold that thought. You might have a bigger problem.

Your parents and family may not see the point of you having a long-distance relationship. They may rant about how it is just a waste of time. They may even tell you that the relationship will never lead to wedding bells.

You know they are wrong. You just need to prove it. You yearn to see the look on their faces when you succeed against all odds. Can you relate to some or all these problems? If you can, then this blueprint is designed just for you.

Why This Blueprint is Your All-in-One Solution

Here is why this blueprint is what you have been looking for. It hands you the keys to a successful long-distance relationship. The mistakes other books make are telling you what worked for their long-distance relationship but not giving you techniques that have worked in many successful long-distance relationships.

To have a successful long-distance relationship, you need to know these keys and master them entirely because each key works together. Like a car that needs all its parts to work in perfect harmony. When this happens, the car is said to have no issues.

I like to refer to these keys as trouble zones. These are the areas in a relationship that are most likely to lead to future issues and maybe even a breakup. Here are some of the keys or trouble zones you need to overcome to have a successful long-distance relationship.

- Trouble zone 1 - Keeping sex and intimacy fun, exciting, and hot each time you are together.

- Trouble zone 2 – How to fit your schedules into each other's timetable and deal with stress.

- Trouble zone 3 - Dealing with trust and fidelity without appearing *'clingy'* and insecure.

- Trouble zone 4 - Handling arguments and disagreements that can kill even the most potent love

- Trouble zone 5 - Effective communication using the phone, texting, video chat, and social media.

- Trouble zone 6 - Long distance dating ideas to keep things romantic and fun

Understanding why these keys are essential and gaining mastery over them will ensure that you have a successful long-distance relationship.

Why You Need This Program

Here is why this program is guaranteed to bring you success. It is diverse. The diversity of topics discussed make this blueprint stand out. Most books that talk about relationships try to fit everyone into the same bucket. That will not work.

People are different. Each person's choice and reaction to things are going to be different. Meaning, the strategies that worked for one couple might not work for your relationship. Reading a couple's love story about how they made their long-distance relationship successful may not help your relationship because you might be a different person.

To make this program incredible and entirely worth it, I have compiled hundreds of successful long-distance couples' success strategies so that you know what works across the board.

These effective success strategies dramatically

increase the chances that your long-distance relationship will be successful. Executing the methods in this blueprint will give you that chance. You do not want to throw that away.

The Life-Changing Benefits You Get from Implementing these Strategies.

Once you follow all suggestions in this program, you will experience the power of looking naysayers in the eye and saying, *"I told you this would work."* There is nothing like sticking your thumb in the eyes of people who did not believe in you.

Be prepared because people are going to say negative things about your relationship. Naysayers are going to try to put down the person you love. Most times, it is all down to jealousy and envy. This expression of jealousy is especially true if the person you love is sexier and more intelligent than the person they are currently dating.

Digesting this blueprint and implementing its strategies will transform your life and leave your naysayers speechless. This blueprint will allow you to enjoy some of the perks of having a successful long-distance relationship.

One of them is improving your communication. Communicating in a long-distance relationship will mean talking via video calls and other methods. Some of these methods you probably never tried before.

Another benefit is that it solidifies your relationship before you both are in the city. Imagine how strong that sort of relationship can be!

Finally, but not least, you get to show everyone that the impossible does not exist in your dictionary. If you can make this relationship successful, you will love your partner much more, and their love will also deepen for you. This blueprint offers you the complete guide to achieving all this and much more.

Helping Couples Have a Successful Long-Distance Relationship

You might be thinking you have probably heard this all before. What exactly can this blueprint offer you that you have not heard of before? That is a valid question. I will not answer by spouting a bunch of words. I am going to give you valid proof from others regarding how my strategies have benefitted their relationship.

Here is what they said.

> *"Hey, Christopher, thanks for the advanced copy of 'Long Distance Love.' Using the strategies in your program, I greatly improved the connection to my girlfriend, who lives in LA, while I live in Denver. She feels the deeper connection as well. We were having some trust issues with the distance, but chapter 6 in your program smoothed out the bumps."*

Austin Zubrin – Denver, CO

"Got your advanced copy via email. Read the entire program in 1 hour or so. I just could not put it down, so much juicy information about keeping sex and intimacy fun and exciting to keep your long-distance relationship alive. Most other books I read never talked much about sex, but your program delivered honest facts."

Meghan Birchdale – Blue Ridge, GA

Now is the chance to take charge of your relationship and virtually guarantee its success. Implementing the strategies in this blueprint will work magic on your relationship.

Your Long-Distance Relationship Will Grow

Here is what I can promise you after digesting this blueprint. This blueprint lives up to its title and subtitle. You are moments away from opening the blueprint for having a successful long-distance relationship.

I can promise you that your connection will be fun and exciting. I can promise you that even if friends and family tell you that your relationship will crash and burn, it will not if you follow what I reveal on these pages. Do not give up on something beautiful.

I am not just saying this. I am confidently telling you what readers have told me. Here is what others have said about this blueprint.

"Opened your advanced copy of 'Long Distance Love' and just want to tell your potential readers what a great resource for anyone starting or currently in a long-distance relationship. Many books often overlook your chapter about sex, but you reveal the truth about how humans feel and how sex keeps a couple connected."

Keith Gaylord – Franklin, TN

If you cannot take my word for it, take theirs. This program promises to be an epic read.

Not Getting This Program Can Be Disastrous for Your Relationship

If you do not buy this program, read it, and follow what I suggest, to be blunt, your long-distance relationship might be in peril. I must be brutally honest with you at this point.

If you do not get this program today, you may very well lose the long-distance love you have now. I have seen it happen too often. Someone just *"thinks"* they know enough about relationships. They try to do it all by themselves.

It never ends well.

Couples that live in different cities, states, or countries have a unique set of problems and challenges that require careful management. Relationships that you had in the same town are QUITE different from a long-distance relationship.

The person you love can easily find someone else attractive in their city. The key to preventing this is by keeping your relationship moving in the right direction. You must be in your partner's heart and mind regularly.

You must consider the distance, and how this impacts the issues, you will have with your partner. These issues can quickly drift into arguments and resentment. Arguments and disagreements are more challenging in long-distance relationships. These confrontations can infect your relationship like cancer and remove all sense of peace you thought you had.

Trust will also become a huge issue. Let us face it; you are not there to see the smile on your partner's face when they talk to you. You can quickly lose trust in your partner. Thoughts of cheating can crush your relationship like a bug.

You also must contend with boredom. Boredom can quickly suck the energy and love out of your relationship like air leaving a balloon. No one wants to experience boredom in a relationship.

I know you do not want to become a stranger to someone you have grown to love with every fiber of your soul. To avoid these nasties, you need to buy this program. Getting this program will ensure that you avoid disaster.

It is Now or Never for Your Relationship

Frankly, it is time for you to decide. Your relationship is at stake, and what you decide next will determine how it goes.

If you choose to keep looking for relationship advice on the internet, you will get bits and pieces that seem helpful. However, you will never get the complete picture to keep your long-distance relationship intact.

The internet is full of people and opinions. How can you pick the good ones while ignoring the terrible ones? Are you willing to put your relationship through that sort of risk?

Here is a better option. You can do what many intelligent people have done and get this blueprint. It shows you all the trouble zones that often crush long-distance relationships.

Chapter 4 focuses primarily on your sex life in a long-distance relationship. I will discuss how improving your sex life can be vital to any form of success in these kinds of relationships.

This sex chapter is an important one. Most books do not want to touch on the topic of sex. However, downplaying the role that sex must play or even ignoring the subject altogether will lead to some severe issues in your relationship.

Every topic in this blueprint provides you with actionable steps to be one of the lucky few couples that move their long-distance relationship forward. These steps can act as a checklist as you gradually improve your relationship.

The key here is not just to glance-over this blueprint. It is more about implementing the strategies. Having the knowledge contained in this blueprint but doing absolutely nothing with it is not very sensible.

You must implement in your relationship what I reveal. You must learn these strategies by heart.

Following my suggestions will lead to growth in your relationship. You can prove to your friends and family just how wrong they were when they told you that your long-distance relationship would not work.

You have much to lose if you stop here without going further. You can make your relationship stand firm like a fortress even if you both live in different cities, states, or countries.

Soon enough, you will be united in the same city. That will be a dream come true. If you want that, you must dive into this blueprint today. Your entire relationship might just depend on this single purchase.

Now that you know why this blueprint is the answer to all your problems, 1 am excited to see you in my next chapter, where I reveal how to have the right mindset for a successful long-distance relationship.

See you in the next chapter!

CHAPTER 1: HAVING THE RIGHT MINDSET FOR A SUCCESSFUL LONG DISTANCE RELATIONSHIP

You are going to face problems in any relationship. It gets more complicated when dealing with long-distance relationships. While being in a long-distance relationship is scary to many people, it's entirely achievable. Get the steps right, and you can have the perfect relationship.

The first thing you need to improve is your mindset. Your attitude plays a vital role in any success you wish to achieve. If you enter into a long-distance relationship with doubts on your mind, then that relationship is already doomed from the start.

This chapter focuses on how to cultivate the right mindset if you are in a long-distance relationship. I also plan to show you how you can enjoy the intensity of such a relationship.

Being realistic about relationships will also be the focus of this chapter. This realism will help you build a long-lasting relationship.

First, let's look at what conditioning your mindset entails

Conditioning Your Mindset

Your attitude towards long-distance relationships will influence the future of that relationship. Changing one's mindset is never easy. However, I have outlined some easy ways to do this. If you want your relationship to succeed, this is one area you need to work on immediately.

1. Changing your thoughts

Your mindset is all about your thoughts. In long-distance relationships, it's common for doubts to infect your mind. Feelings of distrust and fear can quickly eat away at the inner-core of the best relationships. Negative thoughts mainly drive those feelings.

To fight this problem, you need to change your thoughts. Start thinking about positive things. It's best if you say positive things to yourself. After all, we tend to express feelings that we have deep in our hearts.

Thinking positive thoughts doesn't happen instantly. It takes time. However, the faster you start, the more likely you will strengthen your bond with your partner.

2. Understand the psychology

For most situations we face today, there is a pattern.

We need to know how it works. Knowing success patterns is the key to making sure your long-distance relationship works. A successful long-distance relationship depends on the essential core values of trust, commitment, and mindset.

These core values depend on each other. Once you stop trusting your partner, your mindset starts to change. Once your mindset changes, your commitment starts to waver. Soon, you will find yourself feeling attracted to someone else. The same thing can happen to your partner.

You must understand how each misstep leads to another blunder. It helps if you understand the effect that errors have on your relationship. Understanding this will help you keep your thoughts in check, and once you know how missteps play off each other, you can stop the entire domino effect.

Remember that having the right mindset is not a job for one person. Both of you must invest heavily in the relationship. The heavy investment from both of you increases the chances of success. If your effort is at a level 9 and your partner's effort is at level 2, the relationship cannot last. Make sure that your partner wants this long-distance relationship as sincerely as you want it.

Enjoy the Intensity

Keeping the relationship intense is essential. It makes

things spicier. It also keeps both partners interested and longing for each other. The need for passion is not different in a long-distance relationship. If you think your intensity has to reduce in long-distance relationships, think again.

The intensity in relationships comes down to your emotions. Long-distance relationships mean you hardly get to see your partner. Little things such as hand-written letters can spark the intensity levels. Remember the cliché statement: *"absence makes the heart grow fonder."* You are going to miss your partner. The feeling of missing them also allows you to dream about the time when you will reunite. This longing can keep the intensity up.

Another way to keep the intensity flowing is your communication levels. In a long-distance relationship, you will need to communicate a lot. Talk to each other about anything you can think to discuss. These small discussions build trust in powerful ways you never thought possible.

Also, make sure that you share small parts of your day with your partner. By doing this, both of you will feel part of each other's day. Taking pictures or making a quick video when you're out doing errands, shoveling snow, raking leaves, walking to the store, etc., can be of tremendous help.

Enjoying the intensity of a long-distance relationship is one way to keep the doubts and fears out of your mind.

Find Ways to Keep the Love Burning Intensely

When you said yes to this relationship, you probably knew it would require work to keep it going. You were right. It involves effort and sacrifice. The good thing is that you probably won't see it as work or as a chore because you are in love with this person.

In long-distance relationships, keeping love burning is the key to success. Take time to educate yourself regarding how to achieve this. To help you reach your goal, I want to give you a few pointers you will find helpful.

Talk About Your Relationship

You want to remind yourself about how exciting your relationship is. Take the time to talk about your relationship with your partner. Tell them what you love about them. You can also talk about what you found attractive about them. Make sure that your partner is aware of how much you miss them. Reminding your partner that you think about them can make all the difference in your relationship.

Resolving Conflicts

Most couples find it easier to resolve any conflicts they may face in person. So, what if your partner is miles away from you? There's no way out. You have to learn how to address problems remotely using the phone and video chat, never via text.

Most couples eventually break up or end their relationships because they failed to address minor issues. Don't wait for conflicts to pile up. Don't think you can keep it all in until you see your partner. By then, it might be too late.

Learn to improve your communication skills when dealing with conflict. Find a perfect way and time to discuss these issues. Most people find video calls to be especially helpful. It allows you to see your partner's face and emotions. It's the closest you will get to seeing them in person.

Support Your Partner's Achievements

Being hundreds *(maybe even thousands)* of miles apart doesn't mean that you cannot be there for your partner. Your lives go on even when in different cities. Your partner will probably achieve so much when you are not there. They might also face a lot of issues.

You have to show them that you are there for them. Of course, you have to understand that people are different. So, *'support'* might mean and be shown in various ways depending on your partner's preferences.

For example, when facing an issue, some partners might need emotional support. Some partners, on the other hand, might want you to offer solutions to their problems. It's your partner, so talk to your partner and make sure that you know what they want. Doing this will surely help both of you to keep the fire burning brightly in each other's hearts.

Embracing the Reality

Having the right mindset also means accepting the realities of being in a long-distance relationship. While you can certainly improve things between you and your partner, you have to remember it's still a long-distance relationship. So, don't expect things to be precisely how you picture them.

If you don't learn to be realistic about your relationship, things can quickly become very draining and irritating. Here are some realities of being in a long-distance relationship and my recommended steps to deal with them.

Getting Bored

While the intensity of your relationship is critical, boredom is always just a step away. It stems from not seeing your partner up close. While boredom is perfectly acceptable, the danger is embracing the boredom.

You want to have goals in your life. Issues and resentment build when one partner builds their life around the other partner. Make sure you make friends and also have fun when your partner isn't with you.

You can also try to take your mind off the absence of your partner. Take up a hobby that you're passionate about. That way, you can develop yourself while keeping your relationship interesting because now you have more to share with your partner. You're killing two birds with one stone.

Having Conflicts

There's a common myth that the number of conflicts you face when you're in a long-distance will be significantly less. As I said, it's merely a myth. You can expect the same number of problems or even more. The only difference is that they will be a unique set of issues. So you have to come to terms that you are going to have conflicts.

These conflicts will mainly hover around trust, communication, and doubts. You want to find time to address these issues. Randomly reassuring your partner of your love is also an excellent way to reduce problems. Regardless of your efforts, you will have disagreements. Prepare your mind to rise to the challenge.

Communication Issues

Communication is so under-rated. It is the central pillar of any relationship. Take it away, and you will have a big problem. Communication issues are even more critical when you are dealing with a long-distance relationship. You are not going to see your partner often.

You will have to rely on text messages, video calls, and in extreme cases, social media to stay in touch.

It gets even worse if your partner is in a different time zone. The time you have together decreases significantly. There will be missed calls, unanswered messages, and missed online dates together.

You have to be ready and realistic about this. It's going to happen. What is uncertain is how you are going to handle it.

Missing Physical Intimacy

Yes, the *'sex'* word. Having physical intimacy is one of the most critical parts of a relationship. That's why there's a whole chapter in this program dedicated to sex. It's a certainty that you will miss it in a long-distance relationship, and so will your partner.

You have to face the reality that your partner will not be there to give you hugs, massages, kisses, or a swat on your rump after a hectic day.

You might not have a physical shoulder to cry on at night. While you can keep intimacy hot and exciting when you are together, you must prepare for weeks or even months without it.

Your relationship is never going to be the same as having that person in the same city. Understanding this will help you deal with issues when the chips are down.

The Ultimate Reward

While the realities of long-distance relationships might not be ideal, it can be enriching. A long-distance relationship strengthens your bond with your partner. If you can make a long-distance relationship work, then you should be set for success for a long time.

The key, as always, is having the right mindset. It's easy to have unrealistic expectations. It's easy to get discouraged. However, you have to remain level-headed throughout. It's the only way your relationship can keep moving forward. Long-distance relationships can work. It's all up to you and how much you BOTH want it.

Your attitude matters. That has been made clear. With the right attitude in life, you can achieve so many things. It is even more critical when it involves your relationship.

Long-distance relationships have a high rate of success. However, that success often depends on the people involved. Once you cultivate the right mindset, a marriage could be on its way. Without the right mindset, your relationship will probably hit the rocks.

Also, having the right mindset means that you remain realistic about the challenges you will face. Instead of assuming things will work smoothly, be ready to dig in and fight for the love you want. That is the first step in having a successful long-distance relationship.

If you agree that having the right mindset for a successful relationship is essential for success, I just know you will enjoy some real-life stories to touch your heart and prove that long-distance relationships can be successful when you do the right things.

See you in the next chapter!

CHAPTER 2: REAL STORIES TO TOUCH YOUR HEART AND HELP YOU BELIEVE IN LONG DISTANCE LOVE

You are about to enter into a long-distance relationship *(or currently in one)*. You might feel panic and fear. Naysayers are all around you and may not believe that long-distance love works.

Let me assure you that it is normal to have fears and doubts. Long-distance love will need a lot of faith and trust in your partner. However, I want you to know that long-distance love works.

There are thousands of actual stories out there of long-distance love that will melt your heart. There are a lot of reasons why you should read these stories. First, they offer motivation.

They help you believe that long-distance love is possible. Secondly, they provide much-needed insights on how to cope with such a long-distance relationship. While everyone is different, you can draw good ideas to apply to your situation.

So, in this chapter, let us look at real stories regarding long-distance love. To make sure it is all-encompassing in terms of culture, we will not just focus on the United States.

Instead, let us look at stories from all over the world. We will also look at long-distance relationships involving couples with children from a previous marriage.

At the end of this chapter, I can assure you that your confidence will rise like never before.

Real Long-Distance Love Stories from the United States

First, we start with the United States. The United States is a large country. Some of these states are in two different time zones. Therefore, a long-distance relationship in this country is possible. Let's consider some touching stories.

Yasmin and Abdulahi

Abdulahi lived in North Dakota, while Yasmin resided in North Carolina. Their relationship kicked off in 2019 when they met online on a social media platform. Yasmin says that soon, they could not stop talking to each other. I dare say it was like love at first sight.

While the time zones were not far apart to affect their communication, it didn't change the fact that they were so many miles away from each other. By July of that year,

Abdulahi came down to visit her. Yasmin describes this visit as an incredible period in their relationship.

For her, the one thing that helped them was their views and values. They were compatible with each other. Their similar beliefs and values made things smoother in the long run.

Things kept going smoothly, and soon enough, something big happened in October. He came down to visit her, and he proposed. While reflecting on that day, Yasmin admits that it came early because of their culture and background.

However, their wedding plans crashed because of the Coronavirus (COVID-19) pandemic. What also made things challenging was that flight prices skyrocketed.

While they felt the distance's impact, they were comforted knowing that they had a date in mind to live in the same city. Setting a hard date helped them not to get too sad.

Their marriage finally happened after one year of meeting each other and dating long-distance. While the couple would have preferred a larger wedding, they were more than happy to transition their long-distance relationship to the same city!

This long-distance relationship produced more joy for this couple once they started to live in the same city. Their determination to be with each other paid off despite living in different states.

Ryan and Rose

Ryan and Rose met in college in 2009. They met up again in 2019 and started dating. Ryan was in Los Angeles while Rose lived in NYC. That is a 3,021-mile distance and a 3-hour time difference.

To help keep their long-distance love exciting and stimulating, they talked a lot. Most of their discussion was through video chats. They also watched Netflix shows together a lot. Even during the show, they spent a lot of time texting. While they did lots of activities together *(virtually)*, they still made time for their social circles. They regularly went out with friends in their respective cities.

Ryan admitted that the distance was hard to accept sometimes. The hardest part, according to him, was being apart for months after visiting each other.

He mentioned their 10-day trip together and how heart-stopping it felt to go back to normal *(3,021-miles apart)* after spending so much time together. Sometimes, they did not see each other for more than 2-months!

However, the distance did not stop their relationship from growing. Ryan and Rose loved each other so much that Ryan made plans to move to New York.

They lived separately in NYC for over a year before moving in together. The couple proved that one of the best ways to keep a relationship moving in the right direction is by communicating regularly in various ways.

Real Long-Distance Love Stories from Europe

Nina and Jose

Nina is from the United Kingdom, while Jose is from Spain. She admitted that she met the love of her life when she first saw Jose. They met because of her job in the European parliament, which took her to Spain. Long-distance love loomed when she left her job and moved to Lebanon.

This new long-distance relationship sparked a fury of movement. She first moved to Syria while he did his MBA successfully in Spain. After her volunteering ended in Syria, she then moved to London while he moved to China.

To her, it seems that they were always doomed not to be in the same place together. With no plans on keeping things moving in the right direction, this took a toll on their relationship.

After experiencing one breakup, they finally decided to get married. After the couple married, they promised each other that any distance would have to be temporary. They also promised that there would always be an end date in sight before any distance was agreed upon.

Their relationship shows the importance of making promises to each other and keeping them to build trust. Things can quickly fall apart if you don't. It's also pretty clear that having a start and end date in mind helps in long-distance relationships. While coping with the distance is admirable, the long-distance should not last forever.

John and Cathy

John and Cathy met in Wales *(part of the United Kingdom)* in a hotel. Cathy lived in Australia. They did not immediately start dating. After a few years as friends, they finally decided that they were attracted to each other.

They started dating in 2014, and things moved pretty quickly after that. John admits that perhaps being friends first gave them the proper foundation to build their relationship.

To keep the relationship growing, both made flights across the world, especially to Melbourne and London. Their long-distance relationship didn't reduce the spice in their relationship.

They made time to talk to each other online, primarily through video calls. However, at the end of 2014, they finally decided to live together. They first lived in Melbourne. Then, they moved to London and back again.

To be in the same place, they knew that certain things had to fall in place. John had a tour company that needed his attention. He needed to secure a partner's visa to top it off, which cost close to $10,000. That was quite an obstacle for them. However, they found a way around it. John moved his touring company to Australia!

By 2016, they got engaged to each other, and the next year during winter, they were married. John admits that while they had gone through a long journey to get here, it had indeed paid off in the end.

You can tell that Cathy and John were willing to take on many obstacles that kept them away from each other. John was even willing to move his company to an entirely different country!

Real Long-Distance Love Stories from Couples Who Have Children from Another Marriage

Melinda and Mark

Melinda and Mark's story proves that a long-distance relationship can work even if there are kids from another marriage.

They first met in 2006 while they were both married to other people. Their sons were in the same elementary and high school and were good chess players. Playing chess allowed them to play in various tournaments around the country. Melinda lived in South Florida during this time.

So, while their children played chess, they would get to sit side by side and chat. Nothing blossomed from such discussions as both of them were married at this point. They mostly talked about chess and their kids. They soon lost contact with each other.

In 2009, things took a different turn. They started talking again through Facebook. During this period, they were both having issues in their marriage. Melinda was getting divorced while Mark and his spouse were already separated.

During this period, things got a bit heated on Facebook. However, nothing kicked off as both of them kept in touch several times. While Melinda picked up her son from a chess camp at his university in 2013, they again ran into each other. Mark was there as the photographer for the chess tournament.

He saw Melinda across the street, reversed, and came over to say hi. Melinda said that everything changed when they hugged. From then on, the relationship kicked off.

Of course, their relationship required a lot of work after their romantic relationship started. Fortunately, Mark and Melinda realized that and made efforts to make things work. So, they committed that they would see each other at least once every six months.

They both agreed that if they do not see each other that often, their insecurities would consume them. The distance never interfered with their communication levels. They would chat and video call using skype or other social media platforms.

What struck her about the long-distance relationship was the need to talk about every issue. It built trust and communication. There was no physical intimacy or sex to solve a problem. You just had to talk about it, period! Melinda and Mark understood what they needed to do to keep their relationship moving in the right direction.

What You Can Learn From these Touching Stories

I gave you these stories to inspire you. Whether you reside in the USA, South America, or Europe and your partner resides in the same country, but a different city or in a completely different country, you can make long-distance love work and transition to the same city together at some point. Here are some things we should consider after hearing some of these beautiful stories.

Every relationship is different

Every long-distance relationship is different, meaning that what works for one couple might not work for another? Each relationship is influenced by background and culture. The age of both partners can also affect the chances for success or failure. So when considering what works for your relationship, you must keep this in mind.

Communication and trust is everything

When it comes to a long-distance relationship, communication and trust are everything. You have to trust your partner and be able to make certain sacrifices for them. It might also help to discuss a transition date for your long-distance relationship to convert to the same city. Having such a discussion and being completely honest with your partner is the only way forward.

Your relationship will have issues

You have to realize that long-distance relationships will experience conflicts. Sometimes, it might lead to a breakup. However, if you want to be with this person, you will not give up, and neither will your partner. If both of you put in the effort, then problems are manageable.

Long-Distance relationships work

So, what is the conclusion of these inspirational stories? Long-distance love certainly can succeed. Do not listen to what the naysayers have to say. Trust in your heart and your efforts. If your partner is committed to making the relationship work, you should put in the effort as well.

If you enjoyed these real-life stories, it is time to give you a few statistics regarding long-distance relationships; the good, the bad, and the ugly.

See you in the next chapter!

CHAPTER 3: LONG-DISTANCE RELATIONSHIP STATISTICS

Our journey throughout this program has been blissful so far. It probably has filled you with so much joy and hope. That's fantastic. However, it's only right we look at some raw facts to support our claims regarding long-distance relationships.

To make sure you understand the complete picture, we will have to consider these statistics from every possible angle. Just looking at positive statistics will create a skewed view. The same applies to observing only negative statistics.

I know I just painted a rosy picture of long-distance love. If I didn't tell you about some realities, that would be unfair to you. Let us discuss some statistics regarding long-distance love. Remember that once you follow ALL the suggestions in this program, you will significantly increase the chances that your relationship will be successful. In this chapter, we will look at three major categories of statistics.

We'll first look at statistics that will fill you with hope and confidence. Positive statistics to keep you hopeful. The next set of statistics will be genuinely concerning.

They will make you pause and think hard if a long-distance relationship is really for you. These statistics will help you remain realistic moving forward. The last set of statistics are even worse. We're going to examine the very worst that can happen in a long-distance relationship.

I believe that it is always a good idea to start with good news. Having a long-distance relationship has its perks. Evidence supports this fact. Sit back and enjoy some of the most exciting statistics available on long-distance relationships.

You Have a Small Army Backing You

If you are involved in a long-distance relationship, you can rest assured that you are not alone. More than 3.8% of the United States' total population are currently involved in a long-distance relationship. That brings the amount to about 14 million people!

Incredible right? A large portion of these couples are actually in the army. In fact, 2.5 million couples have at least one partner in the military. You are not alone!

Long-Distance Relationships are More Satisfying

While most people will have little faith in your long-distance relationship's success, you are actually on the winning side of the equation. On average, research has shown that long-distance couples experience higher levels of satisfaction. This statistic is a fact because long-distance relationships give couples the chance to build trust and commitment.

This level of trust and dedication can be higher than same city couples because of the amount of work that builds this level of security. So, if you thought the level of satisfaction would be less, think again.

Marriages in the United States Have a Connection to Long-Distance Relationships

If you live in the USA, there's a good chance that you know a long-distance couple. In fact, at the time of this writing, 9.8% of all relationships in the USA began as long-distance. This stat does not include the number of people who experienced long-distance relationships at specific points in their lives.

If you are in a long-distance relationship, there's a big chance that your relationship will outlast the distance of most relationships that started in the same-city. In fact, two out of three couples are likely to continue the relationship because they eventually move to the same city.

The love and trust that they have built over time are enough to transition their union to a same-city relationship with stronger bonds. Surely, that is something you would love for your relationship!

Long-Distance Can Compete With Same-City Relationships

Do you feel that your relationship is under more pressure because you are far away from your partner? Maybe that's true. However, your relationship can still be as solid as a rock. According to statistics, long-distance relationships are just as likely to succeed as same-city relationships.

If you ever feel afraid of the direction your relationship is heading, remember this statistic. That should give you hope.

How likely is your long-distance relationship to last?

More than 60 percent of all long-distance relationships transition to the same city. 40-percent are going to fail. Out of that 40%, more than 37% are likely to end during the first 3-months. Here, the definition of success is the transition of your relationship to the same city.

These numbers might be encouraging and should offer you hope. If your long-distance relationship passes the 3-month milestone, it's more likely to succeed. Now, these statistics probably made you smile, but let us move on to something a bit different.

Statistics that Will Make You Pause With Concern

I just gave you the rosy picture of long-distance relationships, but everything isn't so great. Some challenges can crush the relationship. Trust and feeling secure requires your partner to give you reasons to sleep well at night.

Long-Distance relationships can be a lot shorter

Long-distance relationships, when put on the same scale as short-distance relationships, tend to last shorter in duration. The average time for all long-distance relationships is less than 3-years. Other relationships usually last for about 8-years.

While this statistic might be concerning, it stresses the need to set a date to transition the long-distance relation to a same-city union. The longer the relationship stays long-distance, the more issues you might have to battle. View your distance as temporary and plan to transition to the same city; otherwise, prepare yourself for being single again.

Intimacy issues

Sexual intimacy is a big part of every relationship. Lack of intimacy is not usually a problem in a same-city relationship because you can see your partner several times a week for plenty of intimacy. However, in long-distance relationships, it can be a genuine concern. More than 66% of all long-distance couples say this is a big problem for them.

Out of the 66%, one-third say that not having sex was the most challenging part of their long-distance relationship. If you have faced this issue before, you will benefit from chapter 5 of this program. Yes, I talk about sex because we all want to be touched, if you get my hint.

While this statistic is worrisome, there are ways to combat this issue. One of them is scheduling time to visit each other at least 4-times a year, perhaps even more.

Higher levels of jealousy and doubts

We have already mentioned how trust and fears can quickly erode a long-distance relationship. Well, we have the statistics to back it up this time. Statistics show that more than 24% of couples use technology to stay in touch.

While this might aid their communication, it still leads to a lot of fears. Missed video calls and text messages are among the top reasons why most people get jealous in long-distance relationships. If you text your partner and don't get a return message for hours, you can't help but wonder what they are doing and who they are doing it with.

To combat this problem, you need to understand

each other's schedule and explain when you miss such calls. Your partner will need to know more about your day-to-day, and you need to learn more about theirs.

Problems and more problems

Every relationship has a honeymoon period—that period where everything seems perfect. Couples are more willing to ignore problems during this stage. However, this stage of the relationship is not going to last.

Unsurprisingly, statistics also support this fact. The ending of the honeymoon period also applies to long-distance relationships. Research shows that couples in a long-distance relationship are more likely to face serious conflicts after 3-months. This 3-month point can be a make it or break it moment.

While these statistics are worrying, they are not insurmountable. However, the next set of statistics can very well test your resolve to be in a long-distance relationship. It is about to get rough here, so hold on and stay with me.

The ugly side of long-distance relationships

Discussing the ugly side of long-distance relationships prepares you for when things go haywire, bonkers, or when you get darn frustrated. You will start to believe that all the naysayers were right, and your love cannot last much longer.

Knowing the ugly side better prepares you for how you will deal with these issues. It's better to learn today and create a plan than to allow the ugly side of long-distance relationships to hit you when you are not prepared.

One person is more likely to get heartbroken

In long-distance relationships, one person usually ends up heartbroken because they dedicate more of themselves to the union's success. They daydream more often about when the relationship will transition to a same-city union.

Usually, it is the partner with the most feminine energy who commits themself to endure through the long-distance more so than their partner.

Regardless of your gender, it might be a good idea to consider how you might emotionally handle things not working out. I'm pretty sure you don't want to end up heartbroken, but it is a risk that you must consider.

Communication sucks

It's an open secret that one of the best ways to keep the relationship going is communication. However, what you probably didn't know about long-distance relationships is that communication can suck.

Statistics show that most couples in this type of relationship communicate every 2.7 days. That's a lot of time to pass and not hear your partner's voice! If both of you have hectic schedules and time zone differences, lack of communication can dampen the fire in your relationship.

Sometimes, you don't need to communicate every day. Missing a day here or there is fair. You need a good hour within the day to communicate. This hour of communication will keep you close to each other.

Long-Distance means long-distance

For most people, long-distance might mean 1 hour away. However, the average distance in long-distance relationships is 125 miles. Yours might be hundreds or thousands of miles.

You will need to have a healthy budget for plane flights, bus/train tickets, or highway tolls if you want to see your partner regularly. What if both of you are cash challenged? If one partner is more financially sound, will that person feel comfortable paying for most travel? It might also mean that your time together could be very irregular.

If you do not have the funds to support a long-distance relationship, the emotional distance between you will grow and choke-off the relationship.

High School romances are in for a real fight

High school sweethearts are adorable. More than

75% of all high school students admitted to being in a long-distance relationship at some point. However, statistics are against them staying together after high school once they start college in different cities.

Just 2% lasted past the first year of being long-distance. College presents new avenues to explore and people to date. Some move to other places while others start to work. It might be challenging to keep a long-distance relationship moving in the right direction after high school.

So those are the good, not-so-good, and ugly statistics. These statistics probably made you scared, confident, or even confused. There is good news, though. There are steps to combat these problems to ensure that your relationship survives and transitions to a same-city union.

Guiding Your Long-Distance Relationship to Success

So how do you navigate the challenges of long-distance relationships? I will cover some quick pointers in this chapter, but this program's remaining chapters give you a more in-depth blueprint to follow. Whenever you have a challenge, refer back to the relevant chapter of this program to solve the problem.

Statistics do not influence your relationship

While looking at statistics helps you understand what challenges you could face, it does not determine your relationship's path. It also cannot predict the future. Understand that your relationship is unique. You and your partner hold all the cards and decide how things will turn out.

Have a *'Transition Date'* in mind

A *'transition date'* is when you both plan to live in the same city to continue the relationship. This transition date is the single most significant predictor of success for a long-distance relationship.

You probably have seen this in other parts of this program. It needs attention as early as possible. Have a conversation with your partner about when you both will live in the same city.

Having a never-ending long-distance relationship can take a toll. So, make sure you plan to live in the same city as soon as possible.

Commitments should come from both of you

You have seen the good, not-so-good, and ugly sides of long-distance relationships. You probably know that effort is needed to make your relationship work.

Both partners must commit to making the relationship work even from a distance. Commitment from just one person will not be enough. Decide early if you BOTH are committed.

You have to find ways to communicate

The frequency and quality of communication will be a recurring theme in this program, and that is because it is so important. You must communicate with your partner regularly.

There is no way around this fact. Communicating once every 3-days will not cut it. Mix in audio, video, and text messages, but focus more on video chats. By doing so, you build trust and leave the communication channels wide open.

Statistics are exciting but do not view them as predictors of your relationship. There are so many factors that determine the fate of a relationship. An important one is the attitude of the people involved. With the right attitude, most obstacles can be solved.

If these statistics took your mind on a rollercoaster ride, what I reveal in the next chapter regarding how to handle friends and family who may view your long-distance relationship negatively will calm your fears.

See you in the next chapter!

CHAPTER 4: HOW TO HANDLE FRIENDS AND FAMILY WHO BELIEVE YOUR RELATIONSHIP WILL FAIL

So, you have met someone who lives in another city, state, or country, and you started a long-distance relationship. Your relationship seems to be working out simply fine, and you are thrilled. However, there is a minor roadblock. You have not told your parents or friends about this new person.

Another scenario is that friends and family know that you are dating someone and eager to meet them. However, you have not told them that this person lives miles away from you. You are worried about what they will think.

It is natural to want family and friends to support your new relationship because their support will make you much more confident about your decision to date someone long-distance. However, support from those you care about is not guaranteed. In some circumstances, your parents or friends might not be the biggest fans of long-distance relationships. So how can you handle the situation?

That is what this chapter is all about. Informing friends and family about your long-distance relationship is a big issue for both you and your partner. You might want to pass some of these tips onto them as well. Let us look at this situation from two angles. First, I discuss how to handle the matter with your parents and then with your friends.

Breaking the News to Your Parents

It's time to break the news to your parents. Here is a strategy on how to do it. You may think that your parents will be supportive, but you must prepare yourself for negative comments based on your parents' view of relationships. Parents are two or three generations behind the current dating scene, so their opinion may be skewed against your dating style.

Plan what to say in advance

You might enjoy spontaneity in life. However, revealing your long-distance relationship with your parents should not be a spontaneous event. You need to plan what to say.

Try not to waltz into the discussion without a plan. It can backfire in a very unexpected way. Do your parents have an optimistic or pessimistic view of relationships? Is one parent more positive than the other? The answers to these questions determine if you should talk to both parents simultaneously or separately.

Start with the basics

It's time to tell them the news. It is best if you start with the basics. Focus first on letting them know that you have found someone special. Find a time when they are cheerful to get the most positive reaction.

Keep a mental note of all your partner's strengths. Your parents will want to know what makes this person more unique than the last person you dated.

Keep the fact that your partner lives in a different city, state, or country- away from your parents' ears- long enough for you to first fill your parents' mind with a positive view of your partner.

For now, you want to build a favorable profile of your partner in the mind of your parents. The psychology here is first to get your parents thinking positively about your new partner. Later on, when you say this person lives across the Atlantic Ocean, it becomes more difficult for your parents to say anything negative.

I'm not saying that your parents will not say anything negative. The strategy here is to create an environment where negative comments become more challenging to express.

Talk about distance

Now, it's time to tell them where your partner lives. If you have done the two steps above correctly, your parents will likely know this person matters a lot to you.

So when you tell your parents about the distance, they are likely to be more sympathetic. Your parents will be on your side, and they want to see you succeed.

However, parents are also very realistic. You have to prove to them that you can handle the relationship. Proof might involve showing them how you intend to keep the relationship growing despite the distance. If it is expensive to visit, they will want assurances that you have a financial plan.

Without these assurances, most parents will remain skeptical about your relationship. Once you show them you have a well-mapped-out plan, your parents will have logic to offer positive comments. What else can you think of that will make visitations more possible?

How to Handle Negative Comments from Parents

What if you do all that I mentioned, and your parents still throw negative comments at you? Although it might seem like the end of the world, there are some practical steps you can take to salvage the situation quickly. Let's consider some of them.

Truly listen to their reasons

With alarm bells ringing in your head, the nightmare has arrived. Your parents disapprove. Rather than getting all defensive, this is where effective communication becomes key. For that to happen, you have to first calm down.

Next, try to understand why they don't believe that your long-distance relationship has a good chance of success. You want to listen to them at this point truly.

You might realize that what you thought was disapproval might be some concerns. Try to explain why you think you are making the right decision. With some persuasion, that might be enough.

Tell them that their approval is important

Make your parents feel treasured. You can do this by telling them how much their approval means to you. Tell them how you feel about your long-distance relationship and the impact it has had on your life. There's an excellent chance that your parents will give their blessings after seeing you express yourself clearly.

Follow your heart but listen to the voice in your head

While you might be invested entirely in your long-distance relationship, you also must listen to your head. Your parents might raise some valid concerns that you probably have not imagined. You must understand that this discussion with your parents is not about who is right or wrong. It's really about your future and mental health.

If they have valid concerns, make sure that you analyze what they have said and how you can mitigate that concern. If you detail how you plan to minimize the concern, there is every chance that you will earn your parent's respect and approval.

Next, let's talk a bit about your friends and how you can tell them about your relationship.

Breaking the News to Your Friends

You also want to tell your friends about your new relationship. Generally, dealing with friends is a lot easier than with parents. You don't need to explain to your friends how you will pay for travel, communicate, and grow the relationship. However, your friend will be worried about a few specifics.

These specifics include the genuineness of the relationship. Your friends don't want to see you hurt. They will be worried about your partner's fidelity. Can you trust this new person with your heart when they are hundreds or thousands of miles away?

If you have to explain to your friend why this long-distance relationship is the right move for you, here are some points that might help.

It gives you time for yourself

If you have a hectic schedule each week, explain that

a long-distance relationship gives you time for yourself. Dating someone in the same-city might require three to four nights a week together. Having time to hang out alone or with your social circle is priceless. Every friend will understand this.

Trust is built

Long-distance relationships require an abundance of trust. Such relationships take trust-levels to all-time highs. Trust is something that you must point out to your friends. Having trust improves your self-confidence in the long run and another good reason to go for it.

This person makes you happy

Every friend wants their friend happy. If you tell your friend that your long-distance partner puts a smile on your face, they will find it hard to disapprove. Sometimes, you don't need to tell them because It will be evident from your voice and glow on your face.

What to Do If Your Friends Disapprove

What if your friends do not approve or make negative comments? Some friends do not want to see your life much happier than what they experience. The most negative friends will be those experiencing crappy relationships or those that have always had bad relationships. Here are some tips that will take the sting out of negative comments.

Hear what they have to say

The first step is to hear out what they have to say. When you show a willingness to hear someone's point, they reciprocate the respect to listen to your point. Hearing them out can also open your eyes to some challenges you did not expect. Good friends are out to protect you. If friends disapprove because they have concerns, it is best to hear what they have to say.

Show that you appreciate their honesty

It's not just about hearing them out. It is also about showing that you appreciate what your friends had to say. Showing appreciation means you actually listen to understand and not listen to reply. Make sure you understand what they said. Avoid going on the defensive.

Respond by saying, *'Yeah, that is a valid concern, and I'm glad you mentioned it. That is the reason why we blah blah blah.'*

Doing this will soothe their nerves and give the impression that you have everything under control. You recognized their point, gave thanks, and then explained how you have a plan to solve it or work through it.

Follow your heart

You have to prepare yourself because people will create doubts in your mind. Sometimes, their doubts or reasons for disapproval might not be serious. If you feel that this new relationship is ultimately worth your valuable time and energy, then it is time to follow your heart. While your family and friends are a big part of you, you are the one that decides your future.

Try to avoid creating unnecessary panic for yourself based on the opinions of others. Avoiding panic does not mean that you should dismiss all negative comments. Make sure you have a plan to deal with the concern.

Making the Final Choice

You are the only one who can make the final choice. Your parents or friends may approve or disapprove. However, it's all down to you. When deciding if a long-distance relationship is worth it, there are some simple things you must verify. Here are a few of them.

Make sure that the relationship is real

If you have seen this person face-to-face before, then you can cross this off your list. If you met this person online, you must confirm as soon as possible before telling friends and family.

The best way to verify realness is through video calls. Pictures can be forged. Make sure that you have regular video calls with this person. If they have nothing to hide, this will not be a problem.

Also, make sure that both of you are actually in a relationship together. Don't assume. Make sure your partner also sees you as their exclusive partner. This is especially important.

Consider all objections on the table

Depending on how things go, this new relationship may consume a large chunk of your life. Therefore, you have to be sure that you are making the right call. Do not be afraid to put your long-distance relationship under the microscope.

Considering all objections might mean taking all raised concerns seriously without any sentiment. Understand what each objection means and if the objection might cause damage to your relationship. This process will give you iron-clad confidence that you made the right decision.

Be honest and realistic

Before you decide to tell your friend or parents, you have to be realistic about your long-distance relationship. Realistic includes being honest about the cost to maintain this sort of relationship and the issues you might face. Being realistic will show your friends and parents that you are under no illusion about what lies ahead. That might swing things in your favor, after all.

Your network of friends and family will be your most powerful support system. Without them, it might seem a little lonely. Make sure that you do everything you can to get them on your side. The mentioned tips in this chapter will help you achieve your targets. It is key to having a successful long-distance relationship.

If you enjoyed this chapter about how to handle friends and family who may not believe in the success of your long-distance relationship- I just know you will love the next chapter regarding how to keep sex and intimacy fun, hot and exciting.

See you in the next chapter!

CHAPTER 5: KEEPING SEX AND INTIMACY FUN, EXCITING AND HOT

Like it or not, your long-distance relationship will miss one major thing: sexual intimacy. If you have not mentally prepared for lack of physical contact with your partner, you should now.

Sex and intimacy are essential. The importance of sex is fundamental, regardless of the relationship's age. While many suggest that sex is a small part of a relationship, I could not disagree more. You might devalue sex because the media downplays sexual intimacy as a *'lower form of thinking.'* But as humans, we are sexual creatures, period!

According to The *Journal of Sex Research*, men think about sex 19 times per day, and women think about sex 15 times per day. Most ladies I speak with say that they think about sex every 7-seconds. This difference might mean that people are less than honest on these surveys.

It is crucial to keep sexual intimacy alive and exciting in your long-distance relationship. There are more reasons why this is important. When your relationship experiences unforgettable sex and intimacy, it does more than making things exciting. Great sex and intimacy enhance your relationship's positives and make the negatives seem less of a big deal. You want sex to be fun, exciting, and hot for your partner, especially in long-distance relationships.

Do not think for a second that love alone will over-power the raw sexual drive we all have as humans. Raw sex drive wins every time. If you are not *'ringing your partner's sexual bells,'* each time they see you, their mind will start to wander away from you, and so will their heart. I do not want that to happen.

In this chapter, I show you how to keep sexual intimacy hot and exciting. I reveal how you can discover your partner's sexual desires and how to fulfill those expectations. I also delve a bit into technology and how you can use it to enhance your sexual life with your partner. This chapter promises to be a treat.

How to Learn Your Partner's Naughty Side

You want to find out what your partner likes related to sex. To get this information, you have two options. You can ask them directly. Once you know their sexual wants, it is easier to understand what to do and when to stay within boundaries. The other option requires indirect conversations. Some people prefer indirect discussions because it is less pressure for both.

Regardless of how you find out, you must find out. That is the first step to igniting the sexual life of your long-distance relationship. Here are reasons why you need to prioritize igniting the sexual energy in your relationship.

Keep the spark alive and the relationship together.

A long-distance relationship starts to die once the spark dies. You face a continuous battle to keep the relationship glowing brightly. One of the best ways to do this is by creating sexual tension. Going all dirty and naughty sometimes has the best impact.

Enjoyable sex allows both of you to create a stronger bond.

Good sex gives your heart a good workout and keeps estrogen and testosterone levels in balance. It lowers blood pressure, burns calories, and strengthens body muscles that you did not know existed.

Healthy sexual intimacy shows your partner that you deeply miss them. A deep touch, hug, kiss, spank, or penetrating activity can make your partner feel desired. The feel-good hormones oxytocin, and endorphins, get released during sex. These pleasure hormones create feelings of intimacy and relaxation.

When we feel desired by someone, we feel good and connected to the person who gave us those good feelings. Your regular effort to keep sexual intimacy healthy is a sign of love. Now that we understand the importance of sex let us talk about the act of sex itself. How can you keep your sex life going strong despite the distance?

Best Activities to Spice Up Your Long-Distance Sex Life

Sex is always best in-person. However, you can still do things with your partner, who is hundreds or even thousands of miles away, to release sexual energy in the absence of being in-person.

Virtually releasing sexual energy together also builds sexual tension for when you eventually meet in-person again. I am going to give you several unorthodox ideas in this chapter. You do not have to use all ideas but introduce two or three to your partner.

1. Hot emails can work magic.

If confused about how to start a sexual discussion, turn to emails. An email has uses beyond just business. Start your partner's day with a beautiful sexy picture of you.

Trust me; it is going to stay on their minds for quite a while. Even if you might not be in the best shape, you have a sexy part of you that you like. I do not suggest that you send a dick-pic or a vagina-shot.

What about some cleavage? How about a picture of you wearing a sexy new outfit? It could be lingerie or a fully clothed outfit that shows your curves. Maybe you just got a pedicure or manicure you can show-off with a note saying, *'Just imagine what I can do with these hands.'*

Emails can be a great way to tease your partner with some virtual foreplay. The anticipation for the next email will be enough to drive both of you crazy. Combine this with some kinky gift you mail to them, and your relationship starts to take a new shape.

2. Try phone sex.

Phone sex might sound sleazy. I honestly believe we all have a little *'sleazy'* locked up inside of us. If you cannot express your naughty side with your partner, your relationship may already be doomed.

Phone sex can ignite your sex life. It probably takes your mind back to the 1980s. However, if it does the job, who cares?

While sexting or hot emails can get your mind racing, nothing comes close to hearing your partner saying naughty things on the phone. It is going to be real and have more impact.

Phone sex also comes with its perks. It takes away the physical and allows you to focus on what your partner says. You transform into a better listener. This means that you will be able to listen to your partner without having physical attributes as a distraction.

3. Teledildonic toys might be an option.

Technology has made things more manageable these days. To communicate with your partner, all you need is one app and a mobile device. With the help of apps and some teledildonic toys, you can heighten the sexual experience in a long-distance relationship.

Make sure that you both see each other; as one or both of you use these toys. The effect will be terrific. Your partner will have sexual thoughts about you in their head all month long. Google *'Teledildonic Toys'* for a list of websites.

4. Video calls in sexy lingerie.

Spice up your next video chat together by wearing smoking hot lingerie. You can make it more exciting by slowly putting it on or taking it off during the video call. Imagine your partner's face. Often couples video call each other in casual clothes. Try getting sexy at least once a week.

Do not underestimate the power of the mind. When we see beautiful eye-candy, we want to get our hands on it. You want to get your partner thinking about seeing you again soon.

Make a video call when you step out of the shower and flash your partner a little. Apps and video programs exist to satisfy sexual intimacy. Consider using some of them. To help you decide, I have compiled a list of these apps and their features.

Let us have a look.

The 'Couple App'

Often referred to as the app for two, this app offers real hope to long-distance couples worldwide. It allows couples to share their customized calendar that shows their timelines in detail. It also comes with a feature called the live sketch.

This feature, combined with the thumb kiss, will make you feel like your partner is just around the corner. Just Google this app because there are many versions.

The 'Between App'

Are you a big fan of counting down the days before you see your partner again? This countdown phase can get brutal in a long-distance relationship. The *'Between App'* makes things so much easier for you. This app helps you to remember special dates.

The *'Between App'* operates like a calendar. It celebrates the special days of your relationship and counts down for you.

You can even use this app to chat rather than call your partner to add variety to how you communicate. You do not always need to use your cellphone to chat.

WhatsApp.

This app is popular and nothing too fancy. Yet, it is an incredible way to keep in contact with your partner. I have seen many people survive long-distance relationships with just this app for video and audio calls.

If you have a cell phone plan that charges you per text, use WhatsApp for texting instead. Combine this app with other more fanciful ones to add variety to how you communicate.

We-connect.

With the We-Connect app, you can get sexual vibrations of every kind. The app gives your partner total control of your vibrations. This means that your partner controls the intensity and pressure of the vibrations that you feel. This is a great way to connect sexually in a long-distance relationship.

Tips to Bring Spice to Your Sex Life

I have talked about what you can do to get things moving again. I discussed various apps that can add spice to your long-distance relationship. To help you use these tools properly and effectively, here are some tips on increasing sexual intimacy.

Be open with your partner.

Sexual intimacy is fun when you stay within your

partner's boundaries. Take time to have a conversation about sexual intimacy with your partner. What your partner considers *'kinky'* might seem essential to you.

Do not berate or insult your partner's idea of intimacy. Once your partner knows that you respect their boundaries, prepare yourself for their limits to expand voluntarily over time.

Sexting should come first.

Many ways exist to connect with your partner. If you are just starting out, it is a good idea to start with sexting. Sexting is a great way to begin without feeling too awkward.

It helps partners feel closer despite the long-distance. Once you both feel comfortable with a bit of virtual naughtiness, you can slowly try the advanced tools previously discussed.

Technology is your friend.

While mailing letters the old-fashioned way is attractive in many ways; technology makes it more interactive.

This interactivity is essential with long-distance relationships. Take advantage of the apps talked about earlier in this chapter. Make sure everything goes according to plan. With apps, it is easier to schedule and connect at your best time.

Make sure there is time to talk.

Sexual intimacy is very addictive. It is easy to enjoy so much that it becomes the very center of the relationship. I am sure that you love the exciting rush sexual intimacy brings.

It is still a good idea to put it in its rightful place. Make sure you schedule a time to discuss more serious matters, like catching up with events in your partner's life.

Savor the memories.

Whether you choose photo albums or use technology, make sure you save your sexual intimacy memories. Just make sure only you can find them! Preserving the memories will keep the fire burning even when you are apart.

If you enjoyed this chapter about keeping sex and intimacy fun, exciting and hot- I just know you are going to enjoy the next chapter about managing time and financial disparities when one partner has more of each compared to the other.

See you in the next chapter!

CHAPTER 6: MANAGING *'TIME AND FINANCIAL'* DISPARITIES WHEN ONE HAS MORE OF EACH COMPARED TO THE OTHER

Your friends and family know about your partner, and you have addressed their objections. It might seem that the two biggest challenges to your long-distance relationship are handled. You believe that the relationship is moving in the right direction, or so you think.

However, two significant issues might hurt your relationship down the road if you do not have a resolution. Most couples never think about these issues until faced with them. These problems are time and financial disparities.

Let me go more in-depth regarding both and how to handle each.

The ideal situation in a relationship is that both partners have an equal *(or almost equal)* amount of time and money to spend with each other. The time each possesses will fit each other's calendar perfectly. Each partner would also have the equal financial capacity to travel to see their partner. Who pays for what becomes a formality. What if this is not your reality?

That's why I called it *ideal* in the first place.

You may experience significant disparities in free-time and/or financial capacity. If your long-distance relationship faces this challenge, you need to develop a strategy so that both of you feel that the other is contributing fairly.

A long-distance relationship can be unsatisfying if you feel like you contribute more time and money to keep the relationship intake than your partner.

By the end of the chapter, you will have a strategy to handle disparities in free-time and financial capacity. I also touch a bit on time zones and how they can affect your relationship, and I share with you tips on how to handle the challenge.

Handling Financial Disparities in Long-Distance Relationships

Let me give you a warning about money and online dating. Before you invest finances into any long-distance relationship, make sure that the relationship is genuine. If you met your partner online, you should have had several video chats with this person to convince yourself that this individual is genuine. Money scams are increasing with every passing day. Make sure that your relationship is not one of them.

Handling financial disparities depends on the status of the relationship. If your relationship is new, you both need to understand each other's financial capacity. Do you earn 3-times your partner's income, or maybe it is the other way around? Do you know your partner's cultural relationship with money?

In many cultures, this might sound awkward and scary. Some cultures expect the man to pay for everything, regardless of their partner's wealth. Let me share things you can do to make this process less awkward.

1.   Be as laid back as possible

You do not want to appear eager to know the balance in their bank account. That might give your partner the wrong impression and make them suspicious of you. Stay friendly and a bit laid back when asking.

Try to insert money questions naturally into regular discussions. Discussing money when the topic develops naturally will make your partner more relaxed to share without too much fuss.

For example, if your partner says that they workout at home because a gym membership would break their budget, you just received a signal that they have a low financial capacity. If your partner buys all organic foods and works-out at the most exclusive gym in their city, you just received a signal regarding their high financial capacity.

2. Sharing your financial capacity goes a long way

When you bring up the topic of money, you can quickly add that you will share yours too. That might make things less awkward and take the tension out of the conversation. However, make sure that they share theirs. There is no point in sharing your complete financial picture if they will not share theirs as well.

You do not need to share your income because $100,000 means one thing in New York City and something different in Alabama, Brazil, or parts of Africa.

Share capacity details such as how often you can afford to visit them via plane, bus, or car. Your partner can share the same information with you.

3. Reassure them of your reasons

Make sure that you are direct about why you are asking. Explain to your partner the need to plan for the future of your long-distance relationship. Reassure them that you are not asking for how much they earn. A reasonable partner will understand that a long-distance relationship will have costs involved

What if you are currently in a long-distance relationship?

If you are already in a long-distance relationship, then you might need to take a different approach. Your interactions will probably be less awkward. However, make sure that your partner understands that this is not an interrogation. They can be completely honest with you.

Once you get this topic out of the way, you can start planning. You need to discuss specific issues. Here are some of them.

Flights and restaurants

When you are in a long-distance relationship, your budget must account for travel costs *(flights, bus, train, or car)* and fun events *(restaurants, concerts, events)*. You want to discuss who pays for what and how often.

If one partner comes to the table with a much lower financial capacity, they can contribute in terms of actions. Instead of going out to eat, they can cook for you. Just make sure that the partner with a lower financial capacity contributes somehow; otherwise, one person may feel financially used. You must also consider cultural norms.

In some cultures, the man pays regardless. If you date a person from such cultures, expect friction if you try to get them to contribute financially.

Talk about debts

Discussions about personal debt can be an extremely uncomfortable topic to discuss early in a long-distance relationship. If you can find a way to work the subject into a general conversation, that would make the discussion go more smoothly. It would be ideal to run credit checks before getting emotionally involved with someone. However, just because someone carries debt does not mean that you should not date them.

If at some point you consider marrying this person, a discussion about debt is a must. Someone who may not have been responsible with money in the past may become responsible in the future. Your partner should value financial responsibility. The person you want to avoid is someone who believes that it is best to spend today because you might not live to spend tomorrow.

Talk about savings

Finally, you should talk about savings. Ask your partner about their philosophy regarding savings. Make sure that both of you are on the same page. If you are a saver, but your partner is a spender, you will have many clashes about money. You might not be at the marriage stage yet but realize that one of the biggest triggers for divorce are financial problems.

It might be necessary to have a separate monthly budget for the costs of your relationship. This way, you will know exactly how much you can spend on travel and fun. Each pay period, you transfer a specific amount to this *'love'* account.

Handling Time Disparities in Long-Distance Relationships

You cannot underestimate the importance of finances. However, free time to spend with each other seems to have even more value. Even if you give your partner all the money in the world, there is no relationship without quality time together. You can easily see the problem here.

What if you have more available free time than your partner or the other way around? It is also possible that you both have free time but at different times in the week. You have weekends off, but your partner has Tuesday and Wednesday off. Time zones also create time disparities, and we shall discuss this later.

Here are some tips on how to solve the time disparities in a long-distance relationship.

Find out when you are both free

Grab a calendar and map out when you can make time for each other. The person who has limited free time will need to make the most sacrifices and adjustments. The person with more free time needs to show reasonableness and not expect to have all their free time occupied. The partner with more free time can add activities to fill some of their available time, like volunteer work. There is almost no reason to sit home alone watching Netflix because you cannot see your partner.

Dealing with Different Time Zones

It is time to discuss time-zone issues. If your partner lives in a time zone that is 5+ hours away, finding time for a video chat can be challenging. Let me share some helpful tips.

Find a structure that you both can work with

Usually, I would say to avoid routines because they create predictability, which produces boredom. When it comes to time zone differences, you want a routine. You must create a structure for when to talk. If your time difference is 1 to 3 hours, the difference may not be so much of an issue.

Time zone management is necessary when you have a 5+ hour time difference. This 5+ hour difference can take a toll on a long-distance relationship not planned well. You can do the following:

- Schedule calls ahead of time

- If the call is at an odd time for one partner, setting the alarm might be needed.

- Take turns being inconvenienced. One night you stay up late; the next call your partner wakes up early

Create a calendar so you both know when one stays up late or wakes up early. Both of you should make this sacrifice. If only one partner makes the sacrifice, it might cause resentment over time.

Surprises can be pleasant

Although routine helps you stay in touch when you have a 5+ hour time-zone difference, a little surprise would not hurt. For example, surprise your partner by giving them a call when they can best receive it. Your long-distance relationship needs the occasional surprise to keep things exciting.

Texting apps will help

If you love to chat, using messaging apps can be helpful. While you might not get an immediate reply to your message, sending a text message gives you a chance to express yourself while your partner sleeps. Texting apps like WhatsApp can be helpful if you will not be available for a scheduled call or have a data plan where you pay for each text.

Pictures and videos go a long way

You might be busy for days and not reachable during scheduled calls. You can send your partner pictures and videos to let them know that you were thinking about them. It is a thoughtful surprise when your partner wakes up to a cool video of you doing something the night before.

Maybe you want to show your partner something that you built or started building. Maybe you created some art, made some music, or cooked a great meal. Bombard their phones with beautiful pictures and videos.

Pictures and videos build trust. If you say that you have been busy working on a particular project and then send your partner videos and photos of the project in different phases- that proves that you were indeed working on an important project.

Old-Fashioned ways of communicating

We live in a technology world where we use devices. We forget about how people communicated in the past. If time-zones keep you from communicating with your loved one, the old-fashioned way of sending handwritten letters, cards, and small gifts by mail means so much more. At least once a month, you can try something retro.

Grab some lined paper, a blue inked pen *(not black ink),* and write how you feel about your partner. Express your eagerness to hold them, kiss them, and hold hands in the park again.

Then grab an envelope and a stamp. Yes, they still sell stamps at the post office. If you are under 30 years old, you may have never seen a postage stamp before. Imagine receiving a letter in the mail that you must read. Very romantic!

Things to Keep in Mind When it Comes to Financial and Time Disparities

It can be challenging to navigate these disparities. To help you cope, here are mindset tips you might find helpful.

1. Be patient

The first thing that you develop is patience. Finding an opening to slip in a discussion about finances can be tricky. Once you do, and it feels as if you have a general understanding, do not get angry if your partner struggles to keep their end of the bargain at the beginning. Give your partner time to get better at it. In long-distance relationships, patience is crucial.

2. Be flexible

You must show flexibility. If what you both agreed on is not 100% what happens, be flexible, and see if you can accept the situation. I can assure you that if you both did not discuss these issues and develop a plan; your situation would be more frustrating.

3. Be realistic

If you have had conversations with your partner and

cannot fix the disparities, it's time to be realistic. You have to consider if breaking up with your partner is the best solution. I know you did not expect me to see that, but we must be realistic about what we can and cannot accept from someone we date.

The financial cost and your time are essential factors in any relationship. Make sure you take the proper steps to address these challenges if they exist. Your partner should be as eager as you to use these tips.

If you enjoyed these tips on how to deal with time and financial disparities in your long-distance relationship, I know you are going to love the tips I give you on how to deal with trust and fidelity issues in the next chapter.

See you in the next chapter!

CHAPTER 7: DEALING WITH ISSUES OF TRUST AND FIDELITY, WITHOUT APPEARING CLINGY OR INSECURE

Trust and fidelity are top dogs in any relationship. Without them, you can kiss a monogamous relationship goodbye. This gets more serious when dealing with long-distance relationships.

Partners need assurances of love and trust between each other. When distance stands in the way, it is not always easy to feel your partner's love or trust and that they are honoring their commitment.

Long-distance relationships often suffer from feelings of doubts and fear. These doubts can leave one or both partners feeling insecure.

To solve this issue, you must face the problem. Not doing so will allow it to eat deep into your relationship. By the time you realize the damage, it might be too late.

This chapter will discuss the best way long-distance couples can deal with issues of trust and fidelity. It will also cover how they can do this without coming across as insecure, jealous, needy, or clingy. Finally, we will look at how technology can help you build trust in your relationship.

If this topic interests you, then I am happy to tell you that the answers to your questions lay in this chapter.

The Best Ways to Resolve Trust Issues in Your Long-Distance Relationship

The key to avoiding trust issues in a relationship lies in building trust. It sounds like circular logic, but to have trust, it must be created through your actions. Use the following tips to build trust with your partner.

1. Value your partner's needs

When you value your partner's needs, your partner's trust builds trust for you. When your partner notices that you care about their needs, trust gets built. Sadly, a lot of people do not realize this.

When your partner witnesses that you understand their needs, they feel valued and appreciated. So, what does it mean to value your partner's needs?

First, you want to keep your promises. If you scheduled dates with your partner, make sure to keep them. If you must cancel, do so long before the time and offer an alternative time. Simply put, do not give them a reason to doubt you.

2. Clear honest conversations

There is nothing better than a straightforward, honest conversation. Long-distance relationships need open talk. Open discussions are more critical in stressful situations, or doubts seep into the relationship. Express your sincere feelings to your partner. Doing so will ensure that you keep moving forward.

3. Family and friends

Nothing builds more trust than knowing details about your partners' family and for your partner to know your family. Trust grows deeper if your partner physically meets your family! A virtual meeting is no substitute.

For trust to grow, you both should meet members of each other's family. Meeting each other's friends is also a good idea. Meeting each other's family and friends gives you the sense that you both know each other. Introducing loved ones to your partner builds trust and reduces fears.

Talk to Your Partner Regularly

Speaking with your partner in an open, honest manner and talking to them regularly are two different things. In a long-distance relationship, communication is vital. It can reduce the distrust you might feel for each other. An extended time-period without speaking gives the mind room to imagine many negative possibilities. So, find ways to talk to each other more often. With a healthy level of discussion, trust comes naturally.

How to Handle Insecurity Issues When Your Partner Attends Social Events

Insecurity in a relationship can come from various situations. If you have an extroverted partner, this can increase insecurity issues. Your extroverted partner might enjoy going to parties and other social events. If your partner's extroverted nature fuels insecurity, this is entirely normal. Follow these tips to handle the situation effectively.

1. Do you have reasons not to trust your partner?

I know this is hard, but you must ask yourself if you have a list of reasons not to trust your partner. It is understandable to be insecure about parties and social events. If your partner has not given you any reasons to distrust them, you have the green light to trust them. Feelings of mistrust with zero evidence is called paranoia. Paranoia kills relationships.

If you try to get your partner to reduce their extroverted nature, you risk driving them away. Try to understand that this is their nature. You could show support. That will make your partner happy and delighted dating you.

2. Talk about trust with your partner

It is best to talk about trust issues with your partner. Try to pinpoint what makes parties and social events uncomfortable for you. Could it be the people that your partner socializes with or the activities at those social events?

Be honest about how you feel and try not to attack your partner. Help them understand that this is how you feel about it. Being open and completely honest with how you feel about matters is the first step.

3.   Work together to find a solution

You must work together to find a solution to the problem. Keep ultimatums out of the relationship. You cannot force or scare someone into making you feel comfortable. This is especially true for social events and parties. Perhaps your partner can stop going to particular social events that you find troubling.

Dealing With Trust Issues When You Think Your Partner is Cheating

Feelings of infidelity can take a toll on the relationship. If you believe that your partner is cheating, here is what you can do.

1.   Acknowledge the problem

You are worried that your partner is cheating on you. Denying it does not stop the worry, so acknowledge it. Once you recognize the problem, you allow yourself to work on it. Not recognizing the situation amounts to denial.

2. Ensure that you both share the same definition of fidelity

No one wants to be cheated on. Some people cannot pinpoint what counts as cheating. Ensure that you and your partner have the same definition. Once you achieve this, you avoid misunderstandings.

Maybe you thought your relationship was exclusive, but you never discussed it with your partner. Surprisingly, some people assume monogamy just because intimacy was involved.

3. What signals support your theory?

Do you see signs of cheating? Some cheating signs could be, maybe your partner is okay with seeing you less often; their interest in sex drops, but you have not seen each other in weeks or months; your partner pays more attention to their looks suddenly; they believe that they told you a particular story you know they never told you.

If you have not witnessed a string of cheating signals, you are being paranoid.

The Problem With Being Clingy and Insecure

If you or your partner become too clingy and

insecure, that can destroy the relationship over time. The person exhibiting clingy or insecure behavior rarely believes their actions are harmful. If your partner accuses you of insecure or clingy behavior, look for the following signs that show your partner might be correct.

You have lost your social circle

The more you become clingy, the more likely you will lose your social circle. You begin to base your entire world on your partner. People around you notice and give you space. Just like that, your social circle is gone, and you have only your partner as your entire social world.

Clinginess ultimately puts a strain on your long-distance relationship, no matter how much your partner loves you.

Your happiness is based on your partner

The combination of insecurity and clinginess leaves you at the mercy of your partner. In a long-distance relationship, this can be tragic. Your partner is in a different city, state, or country with their social circle. Never base your happiness on another person. The end-result is heartbreak and many unnecessary conflicts.

Solving Clingy and Insecure Issues

If your partner exhibits clingy or insecure behavior, you must address these issues. First, let your partner know how much you mean to them and that their behavior is probably a result of the distance. The distance may be the root cause. Focus your discussion on the date when both of you will eventually live in the same city.

Help your partner to future-pace about life once your long-distance relationship transitions to the same city.

Ask for your partner's patience and what you can do to help them feel more secure. This little strategy has done wonders for building trust and helping the clingy partner relax.

Clinginess happens for a reason. It means that your partner thinks that they might lose you. Once you reassure them of your commitment to the relationship, the problem goes away, at least temporarily.

Apps that Can Help You Build Trust in Each Other

To ensure that cheating, insecurities, and clinginess do not destroy your relationship, you want to add technology to your arsenal. I talked about apps that can help communication in previous chapters. The following apps can take your trust levels to new heights.

1. Whereareyou App

If your partner just moved to a new country or city, you might find this App exciting. It helps you see the cool places your partner visits. This allows you to share in their experiences. It also reduces worry about cheating in its own way. I call this *'permission tracking.'*

You both should have this App on your phone so that your partner knows your whereabouts. The Whereareyou App gives you lots to discuss during chats. If your partner is faithful, they should be delighted to add this App to their phone to help you feel comfortable.

2. You&Me App

This App features messaging functionality and lots more. It comes with a *'steamed-up'* feature that allows couples to send private pictures to each other with steamy illusion.

Your partner must wipe the screen to see the picture. This adds intimacy and ramps up the anticipation of your next visit together, especially when you have been apart for a while. Using this App is a rollercoaster!

3. Sesame App

If you enjoy sending your partner a gift, the Sesame app makes the process easy and fun. This App allows you to send your partner gifts with beautiful themes. If your partner's love language is receiving gifts, this App is one that you should try.

4. Fix a fight App

If you have ever fought with your partner, you know how much it sucks. Well, not to worry because there is even an app to solve arguments. The fix a fight app gives you expert tips on settling a variety of relationship issues.

Some features help each person to calm down. With this App, you will feel calmer and more inclined to listen to each other actively.

The ability to calm down and listen is crucial in a long-distance relationship. If you want to improve conflict resolution in your relationship, get the Fix a Fight app.

5. The Avocado App

Finally, we have the Avocado App. This App is great if you are looking to connect with your partner on a deeper level. It allows you to keep a joint calendar and exchange memos with each other.

It also allows you to send the stickers with love to your partner. With the Avocado app, the troubles of long-distance relationships seem to melt away, even if for just a moment.

Coping with long-distance involves a lot of steel and willpower. It also involves executing the proper steps and being open. Instead of making accusations, try to talk to your partner about how you feel. Use the apps listed in this chapter to create more intimacy and build trust.

If you thought that this chapter on dealing with trust and fidelity issues was useful, I know you are going to enjoy the next chapter about how to handle arguments and disagreements in your long-distance relationship.

See you in the next chapter!

CHAPTER 8: HOW TO HANDLE ARGUMENTS AND DISAGREEMENTS WITHOUT KILLING THE LOVE AND THE RELATIONSHIP

It is inevitable to experience conflicts in your relationship. If you have not had your first quarrel with your partner yet, you are still in what many call the *'honeymoon stage.'* This stage can last from 10-days to 6-months. So what happens when the first conflict hits? How do you cope with it?

A relationship in peril often experiences inappropriately handled arguments and disagreements. The sad part is that many couples find it hard to navigate conflicts. If you are a couple facing conflicts that often escalate, this chapter is for you.

I show you how to avoid most disagreements in the first place. I also guide you on how to handle disputes when they arise. To make this chapter more practical, I will give you various examples of common conflicts that can take place in a relationship. The key here is to handle problems without killing the love and the blissful relationship you have formed.

Why You Should Handle Conflicts Quickly

Because you have *(or considering)* a long-distance relationship, your conflict resolution skills must be exceptional. Let's consider a few bad things that can happen if conflicts are not resolved quickly in a long-distance relationship.

It could be the beginning of the end

Arguments are normal. However, when left unchecked, they can spell doom for your relationship. Slowly, arguments can lead to other problems such as doubts, distrust, and even resentment. Most couples pretend that serious issues do not exist. Thus, they do not talk about them. You can be sure that the problem will come back to haunt you in the future.

Small arguments are more dangerous

The especially dangerous arguments start small and mild. These arguments are relatively easy to sweep under the rug or shrug off. While some conflicts might be minor, some of them might fester. When not dealt with, other more minor issues accumulate. The result will be a gigantic conflict made up of many smaller layers of issues wrapped in one. Absolutely terrifying.

It destroys your bond

While arguments might not tear your relationship apart, it destroys the initial bond you first developed with your partner. The rush and the spark might no longer be there as well as the motivation to get things moving again. It is not something that you should wish on your relationship.

How to Manage Arguments and Conflicts with Your Partner

Conflicts are typical in relationships. However, in long-distance relationships, it takes a different tone. It can erode trust and intimacy, especially since you do not often see your partner. For this reason, you want to reduce the number of conflicts that your relationship experience. Let us discuss a couple of pointers that can help you reduce disagreements.

1. Your tone tells the story

You are not physically with your partner. When you speak, your partner relies entirely on your tone of voice. The tone you use to talk to them can either aggravate the situation or be a soothing tonic. The right tone can help your partner feel valued and not judged.

This becomes more important if your partner is overly sensitive. Sensitive people are very adept at picking out the changes in your voice and dwelling on them. Trust me; there is nothing that can kill a relationship faster than the tone of your voice.

2. Actually listen

People struggle to listen to one another when emotions rise. Most only listen long enough while thinking of ways to reply. A long-distance relationship necessitates the need for listening on a deeper level than if you both lived in the same city. Listening without any form of judgment or anticipated response will allow you to understand your partner deeply.

When you focus on listening, you can prevent many arguments. So what if you have tried your best to avoid disputes to no avail? Well, you have to learn how to handle disputes better.

Simple Steps on Handling Arguments and Disagreements

Remember that your goal is to protect your relationship from strains caused by arguments. You must learn how to handle disputes bound to arise in your relationship. Let us consider a few ways you can do this.

1. Keep the environment calm and open

A frustrating problem you might face during an argument is keeping the floor open for further discussion. Both partners in a long-distance relationship must express themselves. If you find this hard, check if your relationship is toxic. In relationships where partners respond to genuine worries with passive-aggressiveness, you might be looking at an abusive relationship. To stop your relationship from heading in that direction, both of you must make sure that you both feel comfortable expressing yourselves.

2. Remain calm when things get heated

Discussions and disagreements can become heated. To prevent the argument from disintegrating into insults, one or both partners must learn how to remain calm. Try to avoid using your partner's past mistakes against them in such a discussion. Most couples refer to this as a *'low blow.'*

While trying to remain calm, you must remember how to spot a verbally abusive relationship. If your partner hurls insults or throws swear words at you, then your relationship might be verbally abusive. Analyze things using an objective mind to see if there might be a problem in your relationship.

3. Try to look for a way to make it work

In every conflict, each person has their perspective or way that they view things. Both partners must learn to meet in the middle to make things work. Meeting in the middle means making some sacrifices for the relationship's sake.

It does not mean having to feel like you must give up your entire life for the relationship. Try not to sacrifice your values. The key is finding a way to compromise.

Once you find a compromise, things will be a lot smoother.

4. Choose your battles

While minor issues can fester and infect your relationships' long-term chances, it is essential to choose your battles. You have to consider if this argument is so important that you cannot let it go. I saw a quote that said if something does not matter in the next five years, it should not matter now.

You have to understand that you can never be in total agreement with your partner. If you are, then something is terribly wrong. If you cannot agree on more significant issues, then you must consider if this is the relationship for you.

5. Isolate the actual problem

Treating the symptoms of the disease will not cure the disease itself. It is only going to help with the pain. The same applies to handling conflicts and disagreements. Make sure that you do not treat the results of the problem. Focus on the root cause of the matter. Once taken care of, chances are that the entire issue will be resolved entirely.

6. Accept the reality

Conflicts that repeat themselves can be a sign that your relationship will not work out long term. This is especially true in long-distance relationships. If you have tried everything to reduce arguments and conflicts flare up with shocking frequency, it might be time to accept the truth.

Accepting the truth does not mean you have failed. It simply means that you were strong enough to make the right call despite the blinding power of love. Now, let us look at examples of typical conflicts and what you can say and do to handle them successfully.

Examples of Conflicts and How to Handle Them Like a Pro

There are dozens of potential conflicts that you might encounter. Obviously, I cannot cover every one of them in one chapter. There are a few common snags that almost every long-distance couple must grapple with, and I will touch on them.

Your partner does not contribute enough to the finances

A long-distance relationship means that you must travel to see each other many times during the year. Planning a budget and sticking to it will involve both partners. However, your partner fails to pull their weight. You feel financially used, and the situation makes you resent your partner.

Money is a sensitive topic. It is best to be subtle but

firm. A good strategy is to ask your partner to create the next budget and assign who pays for what next month. Your partner will visually see how little they contribute when they must write your name near most items.

Your partner might agree to pay for more items without you asking them to contribute more. It is one thing to tell someone that they do not contribute enough, but when they see the reality on paper, the situation makes them feel a bit guilty.

If this does not work, you can bring up the matter when both of you are in a good mood. It can be over the phone. However, video calls and face-to-face conversations might be the best approach for this conversation.

If your partner seems hurt by the discussion, make it clear that you only want them to be as invested as you are. Do not attack them about their lack of contributions from previous months.

Your partner does not invest enough time in the relationship

If you notice that your partner does not have enough time for your relationship, the issue could be that you have too much time on your hands and you need to add activities to your life, or your partner should make you more of a priority.

The first thing you must do is to talk to them about

it. Make sure that you are transparent and honest about how you feel. You do not want to attack them for not investing enough time because your partner might not realize how you feel. Another approach is to suggest ways to increase your time together.

Your partner feels that you attend too many social events

This time the issue is about your behavior. Your partner thinks that the amount of time you spend at parties and social events is just over the top and needs to be reduced.

They might believe that your social events reduce the amount of time the two of you could be spending together. To handle this conflict, you must resist the urge to be defensive or to listen long enough just to reply.

Carefully listen to their concerns and empathize with them. While they might not like your parties and social events, you can make some compromises without giving up your activities.

Perhaps you can attend business parties and critical social events. You could also place the resolution in your partners' lap and ask them what they think you should do with your spare time when they are not with you.

Tell them that if they visited you more often, you would have no need to attend so many events, or you could bring them along when they do visit you.

This strategy is a bit aggressive because you want your partner to offer the fix. Of course, they will not tell you just to stay home and watch Netflix.

Final Tips on Handling Conflicts

I could write an entire program about conflict resolution techniques. I have touched on typical issues you might face and how to manage each one. I reserved my best tips for last. Here you go.

1. It's never a war

A relationship is never a war. Make sure that you do not handle it like one. Instead of viewing every doubt or worry expressed by your partner as an attack, see it as a way to improve the relationship.

2. You are still a team

It is not you versus your partner. It is you and your partner versus the world. So, do not make the mistake of pushing your partner aside. Keep in mind that your relationship is a team effort. By realizing that, you will approach each issue with the notion that you are talking to a team member and not the opponent.

3. Give your partner the benefit of the doubt

A cliché, but remember to give your partner the benefit of the doubt. You are in a relationship with this person because you love them. This means that they deserve a little bit of trust from you. When in doubt, choose to trust them. That can make things a lot better.

Understanding how to avoid and handle disagreements and conflicts in a long-distance relationship is especially useful. It can change the direction your relationship is headed. In the next chapter, I discuss effective communication strategies that will keep your bond strong.

See you in the next chapter!

CHAPTER 9: EFFECTIVE COMMUNICATION STRATEGIES TO KEEP YOU FEELING CONNECTED

Have you ever felt disconnected from someone before? Perhaps you had no problem communicating with the person; however, something just didn't seem right. Maybe you did not know each other on a personal level.

Well, no matter what it was, you are right. It is pretty easy to feel disconnected from someone you communicate with regularly. Something more terrifying is that it can happen in a long-distance relationship.

To keep your relationship going strong, you need to stay connected. In-depth communication is genuinely one of the best ways to remain connected. Simply speaking does not count towards feeling connected. Various communication methods can help you to feel a deep connection. This is the main focus of this chapter.

We examine several ways in which you can not only communicate but feel deeply connected. This includes your phone, video calls, and social media platforms such as Facebook. If this is a problem that has been troubling you, prepare to get all the answers you need.

Why Communicating Is Different From Feeling Connected

While communication is essential, it is not the same as feeling connected to your partner. View communication as a set of tools to get you feeling connected. If you misuse these tools, you will not achieve your goal of a deep connection with your partner.

To enjoy that wonderful feeling of connecting with your partner, you must sharpen your tools of communication. This means developing communication strategies that tap into how you feel and how your partner feels.

A long-distance relationship requires that you use communication strategies to help your partner feel like you both live in the same city.

Let's consider one of these strategies.

The Power of Using Your Phone to Feel Connected

Thankfully, technology blessed us with a helpful tool called the smartphone. With it, we can easily communicate with loved ones in distant lands.

The wonders of a smartphone do not guarantee an emotional connection with your partner. Many couples complain that they run out of things to say to their partners. So how can you never run out of things to say?

How not to run out of things to talk about

1. *Don't force it*

Never try to force a connection with your partner *(or anyone)*. Do not call your partner with a well-thought plan of things you must discuss. Let spontaneity guide you. You may be surprised how well this turns out.

2. *Do not just talk about your day; talk about how you felt*

The power to connect lies in sharing your feels about your day, not merely what you did for the day. When your partner shares their day, relate everything back to how their day made them feel. Try not to skip the *'feelings'* part of what occurred that day.

Make it a habit to keep mental notes of the essential things that happened during your day and how it made you feel. You can even make things so much better by taking pictures and videos of things that actually happened. For example, that delicious burger you could not stop eating although your belly was full.

Expressing feelings to your partner and hearing about their feelings not only gives you something to talk about; it strengthens the bonds between you.

As you both express your feelings about the days' events, more topics magically appear. After you get off the phone, you will feel so much more connected to your partner, and your partner will feel a deep connection to you.

3 Ways to Keep Your Relationship from Slowly Dying Out

Do you feel that your relationship is on its last breath? Losing control of conversations or just struggling to find topics to discuss indicates not enough focus on how you both feel about events in your lives. Here are 3-ways to take your relationship to where it used to be.

1. Relive past memories

It is a mistake to believe that you must always talk about something new. In fact, you have a treasure of past experiences to relive. Past memories can keep you talking for hours on the phone. All those good feelings rush through your veins again, helping you both feel emotionally connected.

Discussing past memories does not just give you more time to talk to your partner. It reminds you of how extraordinary your love is for each other. Reliving past memories can get a stalled relationship moving forward.

2. Learn deep communicate

Deep communication methods require that you both know how to communicate to build a connection. It means mastering the act of listening, responding, and expressing yourself so that your partner feels your words.

It also means observing gestures and tones that might denote how your partner feels. Once you know how to communicate effectively, especially over the phone, talking to your partner becomes easier.

3. Try other forms of communication

To keep communication fun, you need to explore other forms of communication. Most communication in long-distance relationships occurs over the phone. Add other communication forms like texting, video chats, and Zoom calls.

Call from different locations: your backyard, in the parking lot, in your basement, etc. Let your partner see you in different environments to add interest to the call. Changing locations prompts additional questions to keep the conversation moving. You also appear as a more exciting person.

3 Golden Rules Of Texting

The aim here is to make sure your relationship keeps breathing. You want your texting game to be fun. Here are tips that can make things exciting.

1.   Early texts are key

The first texts you exchange in the morning set a critical mood. After the mushy texts back and forth, make sure your texts discuss your plans for the day. Are you going to schedule a call for later? Is there somewhere you plan to go that might be interesting?

Discuss your plans with your partner as early as possible. This sets you up for the rest of the day and allows your partner to know what to expect from you.

2.   Do not argue via texts

While texting has its pros and cons, one con is using texting during arguments or disagreements. The simplicity of firing off a text when upset can make matters worse. If your partner misreads the tone of your messages, you elevate a small issue to a large one. If you sense tension while texting, stop and give that person a call.

3.   Make sure there is chemistry

Texting your partner can lead the relationship to a slow death when chemistry dies. Work on feeling connected again. Simply saying good morning or good night will not work here. Make sure you keep things personal. Share what motivates you and encourage your partner to do the same.

Now, let's consider another effective communication method that you should use.

The Power of Video Calls to Feel Closer

Throughout this program, I have mentioned that video calls are simply the best communication form in long-distance relationships. I want to dive into different ways to take video calls to the next level.

Adding sexuality to your video calls through erotic visualization

Video calls are an excellent avenue to keep your relationship intimate and sexual. While adding sexuality through video calls might seem simple, there are a few things to keep in mind. This section is only for you if you feel comfortable adding some kinkiness to your communication.

Discuss it with your partner

Step 1 is to discuss this with your partner. While you might be similar to each other, you each have your likes and boundaries. Try to find your partner's comfort level. For example, your partner might not be comfortable exposing their bodies on a Zoom call. If this is the case, then you need to accept it.

Pick your app

Not all apps allow explicit content. Make sure that you do the appropriate research. You might not be able to use the apps fully as you wish because some apps come with serious rules regarding explicit content. I will not list apps here because the rules of apps change all the time.

Scheduling ahead is best

The best intimacy occurs spontaneously but make an exception this time and schedule this activity ahead of time. First, it gives you time to plan it all out. It also ramps up the tension and anticipation your partner will feel. You never know if your partner will be somewhere less private when you initiate a video call.

Do not be afraid to use your toys

If you are into sex toys and products, do not be afraid to use them. However, it might be a good idea to ask your partner if they are okay with that. Using sex toys can take the whole sexual tension to the next level. Toys such as finger vibrators and clit vibrators will surely set the mood. So, if you have these toys, allow them to make an appearance!

Ramp up the noise

In physical sex or other sexual activities, noise is a good thing. It tells your partner what you enjoy or that you are enjoying yourself. So, when using video calls to send erotic videos to your partner, do not hold back on the noise. Your partner will want to hear your sounds and will appreciate them.

Picture quality matters

Your entire video chat performance might not generate excitement if the camera quality is grainy, blurred, or distorted. You do not want your partner saying, *'Hey, is that your <blank>?'*

A comment like that might kill the mood instantly. The lighting and camera influence quality. You can place your camera or device against a pile of books in a vantage point. Red lighting can work wonders.

Being interactive and not just talking is important

Being interactive is crucial even in a video call. Ensure that you are not merely doing all the talking or vice versa. Make sure you get your partner fully involved in the activity. You are not there just to entertain your partner. You both should entertain each other.

If you achieve this, the results will boost how connected you both feel towards each other. Doing this during a sexual video call will only increase the emotional attachment you feel towards each other.

There is one final thing. Never send out videos to someone you just started dating long-distance. While you might be in love with your long-distance partner, one thing that you should consider is the amount of time you have been together.

Do you trust them? Have they proven to be reliable and honest? You want to reduce the chances of these videos being used against you in the future.

Use Facebook to Build a Deep Connection

Another helpful tool most couples use for their long-distance relationship is Facebook. You are probably aware that many couples met on Facebook. In this case, you will use Facebook to form a deep connection with your partner. Nothing sexual in this method.

Create a private Facebook group

If both of you have mutual and very close friends, you can create a private Facebook group with your closest friends. It will be like hanging out in-person.

Every now and then, you can go to Facebook and have a wonderful conversation. Sometimes, it is not just alone time together that builds deep connections. You can also connect with your partner by connecting with your partner's friends, and then your partner joins the conversation.

An ideal place to chat

Facebook comes with a messenger feature. This means that it is an ideal place to connect with your partner. If other apps like WhatsApp do not cut it for you, Facebook Messenger might be a great place to connect with your partner.

In long-distance relationships, staying connected is enormously essential. The best way to stay connected is through deep communication methods.

The methods mentioned are extensive but not exhaustive. It can be the start of something unique. In the next chapter, I give you some of the best date ideas for couples in a long-distance relationship.

See you in the next chapter!

CHAPTER 10: LONG-DISTANCE RELATIONSHIP DATE IDEAS TO KEEP THINGS FUN

One noticeable thing about long-distance relationships is distance. You will not see your partner for long periods of time. While this often leads to feelings of loneliness, it also presents a beautiful opportunity. You get to spend memorable times together when you do see each other.

So, what about when you are apart? How can you keep the relationship moving along a positive path? The answer to that question could very well be going on dates with each other while in separate locations. How can you plan these dates even when you are apart?

This is one of the issues most couples in long-distance relationships face. That is why I am going to focus on this issue in this chapter. I will also look at some apps that can make dates easier for you and your partner. So, let's jump right into the most important thing first.

The Best Date Ideas to Keep Your Relationship Moving Forward

1. Plan to perform activities virtually

If you are looking for exciting date ideas, nothing beats doing an exciting hobby together. This type of date gives you a lot of options. For example, if you both love baking and cooking, this might be a good option. You can both bake together virtually. Of course, you will have to video call your partner with this kind of date.

Another idea is to have a Wine-Paint night. How about poetry reading together? Use these ideas to develop other ideas. Planning and doing something together will leave you with the feeling that your partner is not so far away after all!

2. A virtual dinner or breakfast

While still on the topic of food, another great date idea is having dinner or breakfast together. You could make the setting inviting and memorable. Let it have the aura of an actual date.

You should both dress up for the occasion depending on what you prefer. Lingerie can also be a great outfit. Make scrambled eggs and toast together in thongs with your video camera capturing the entire meal.

Turn your backside to the camera, bend down to pick something up off the floor in a sexy way, then turn to the camera and say, *"Oops, did you catch that?"* Have a little fun. This idea might not be favorable to couples who live in totally different time zones. However, you can still get it to work with a little bit of imagination.

3. Watch movies together

Watching movies or going to the movie theatre is one of the most common date ideas for people living in the same city. However, that opportunity goes away when you are in a long-distance relationship. Or does it?

Even if you are in a long-distance relationship, there are ways to watch a movie together. So, why not schedule a time with your partner and make it happen. Make sure that it is a movie that both of you totally enjoy.

Some couples have found it easier or more interesting to watch TV shows or a series together. Of course, nothing is stopping you from sleeping off in the middle of the show. Just like old times, don't you think? I am pretty sure that you will enjoy this idea.

4. Play a game together

Another fantastic date idea is playing games together. It does not have to be a serious virtual game. Just make sure it is a game that both of you will enjoy at the end. If you are not into the same types of games, find an activity that both of you enjoy. Make sure that it is one that will give you and your partner good vibes.

5. Video call from a new location

Sometimes a good date idea is the one that stares you right in the face. One such date idea is scheduling a video call with your partner, but from a different location than usual. There is one big reason why selecting a different location is a good idea. It makes you more attractive. The anticipation of where they might call you from can be intoxicating.

You do not need to always video call from the exact location in your house. Try calling from outside, in the back yard, in your car, from some off-beat parking lot, on a swing-set in the park, at a nearby lake, or from some rooftop. Get creative. Doing this will also give you more things to discuss.

6. Read books together

Are you both into books and all the delight that comes from them? If you are, consider adding it to your list of date ideas. Reading the same book or two different books will be a brilliant idea. Now, I am not saying that you should read aloud. You can both read in silence and share some of your best moments with each other. It is an excellent way to relax with your partner and learn more about what makes them tick.

7. Truth or dare

Do you miss the truth or dare games you played in high school or college? You can relive these games with your partner! There are no complex rules when playing truth or dare. You can decide to use an app to develop all the juicy questions, or you can choose to ask them off the top of your head. Truth or dare also allows you to explore intimacy in your relationship. However, that is left mainly for you to decide.

8.   Double dates

Another fantastic date idea is the double date. Long-distance does not stand in your way of going on double dates. You can go on one with a couple that you are comfortable with. It can be over zoom or through other messaging apps. The other couple can be in your same city, but you can all meet via Zoom for the date. To keep things fun and exciting, you can even throw in some games. I can assure you that this will be interesting.

I have given you a bunch of date ideas. However, this list is by no means exhaustive. There are many ideas out there. With some creativity, you might find the perfect one for you and your partner. Now, let's consider some apps which can help keep your virtual dating games on track.

Top Apps That Are Perfect For Virtual Dating

Some of these apps have been mentioned in an earlier chapter. However, I am mentioning them again because these apps perfectly fit this category.

1. Truth or Dare- Dirty Games app

Remember we talked about adding truth or dare to your list of date ideas? Well, how about an app that is fully dedicated to that purpose? If you want an intimate date night, this is one of the best ways to add some spice into your relationship. You get the typical choice of choosing between truth or dare.

2. The Foodie app

Another app that is perfect for a dinner or breakfast date is the Foodie app. This app has a truckload of recipes just lying down waiting for you. As stated earlier, this is the best app to use if you intend to cook or bake together.

The app can also be an excellent place to start when your partner comes to your city for a visit. It shows you all the fabulous restaurants around your city that you can visit. The Foodie app is simply a joy to use.

3. WhatsApp

If you are going for the old-fashioned video call date, you should probably stick to WhatsApp. They have a good video call setting, and their video camera is good on a solid internet connection.

The app has an excellent messaging platform. It is the perfect app if you want to spend some alone time with your partner. Some people find it easier to discover gaming platforms on WhatsApp. It's something you should probably do some research on.

4. The Line app

If you want to have a date with your partner by talking on the phone, you should consider the Line app. It is an excellent way to save your money. Make sure that your internet connection is strong. You can also chat with the Line app. It comes with a complete package.

5. The You & Me app

If there is one app that can directly impact your sex life in a long-distance relationship, it's the You & Me App. If you are planning an intimate date, their steamed-up pictures feature might be the best thing. It presents transmitted photos and videos on a steamed up screen. To see the images, your partner will have to wipe the steam off the screen. That builds anticipation and adds a sexy touch to the whole date.

Tips on How to Keep Your Date Ideas Exciting and Refreshing

We have talked about some exciting date ideas and apps you can use to pull it off. Here are proven tips on how to make it all perfectly come together.

1. Technology is your friend

Apps and other devices can play a significant role in your long-distance relationship. Technology is one of the easiest ways to make your long-distance relationship enjoyable. So, do not be shy about using technology. Utilize technology to the fullest. Using some of the apps that I have outlined above is a good start.

2. Make sure that you have regular date days

When apart from your partner, it is easy to get lazy and stop going on dates together. While you may not immediately feel the negative impact on your relationship, it can slowly erode the bond you share with your partner. When this happens in a long-distance relationship, the consequences are even graver.

Take time to have date days with your partner. The joy you will get from it will keep you motivated and your relationship strong.

3. Remember to have a transition date insight

Although there are different ways to keep a long-distance relationship exciting, nothing beats having an end date in mind. Let's be honest- nobody wants to stay in a long-distance relationship forever. Ensure that you have a transition date in mind and communicate that date to your partner regularly.

By doing so, you can enjoy your dates with the full knowledge that your time away from each will not be forever. Eventually, these date ideas will lose their luster. You want to transition your long-distance relationship to a same-city union before that happens!

4. Take care of yourself

While you are doing things to keep your relationship moving in the right direction, you should also take care of yourself. Having a relationship does not mean that you no longer have your own life. Make sure that you maintain your social circle. Go out and have fun sometimes. Doing so will give you the needed boost to refuel and come back even stronger for your partner.

5. Finally, keep planning

Never stop planning new things to keep your relationship moving in the right direction. Whether you think of new date ideas or find time to visit each other, just keep planning. It makes your partner see how invested you are in the relationship. It also ensures that you maintain your bonds.

In this chapter, I talked about virtual date ideas that you should try. I also discussed various ways technology can help you bring these ideas to life. I personally feel that you should give it a try as soon as possible. It can bring a breath of fresh air into your relationship.

It is also essential that you keep things as romantic as possible. How you can effortlessly achieve this will be discussed in the next chapter.

See you soon in the next chapter!

CHAPTER 11: ROMANTIC THINGS TO KEEP YOUR LONG-DISTANCE PARTNER EXCITED

In every relationship, it is a good idea to keep things fresh. Keeping things fresh is a great way to keep both partners committed and happy. Boring and predictable can leave the relationship facing a rut. Keeping things fresh and exciting is more critical in long-distance relationships.

In long-distance relationships, you will not see your partner as regularly as you want. You will also get consumed in your personal schedule and social circles once in a while.

Therefore, you want to find ways to have your partner thinking about you when you are not there. One way to do this is by doing romantic things for your partner. How on earth can you find romantic things to do when you cannot be near each other?

Well, that's what I am going to discuss with you right

now. To put the icing on the cake, I will also reveal some romantic online games that you can play with your partner. These games will help both of you bond like never before. You both will feel as if the other lives down the street.

Gift Ideas that Say *"I Love You"*

Gifts are often the epitome of romantic gestures. Knowing appropriate gift ideas might be an excellent way to start. Remember that everyone is different. This means that a gift that might work wonders for one couple might not work its magic the same way for you.

Regardless, I am here to provide you with some fantastic ideas to help you get started.

1. Get matching clothes

There is nothing more adorable than seeing couples hold hands and walk down the streets in matching clothes. It shows how close they are to each other. Getting matching clothes might be a great idea.

Many people have found matching hoodies to be perfect. Get matching hoodies and wear them the same day you visit each other. What about matching baseball caps? Wear your hats while having a video chat. I know this might sound nerdy, but quirkiness is a way to bond. Use your imagination and think about other forms of clothing.

2. Send them flowers

The old-fashioned ways of showing love still live today and can be utilized in long-distance relationships. One such old-fashioned way is by gifting your partner flowers. You do not need to wait for Valentine's Day to give flowers. You can make giving flowers interesting on any day.

Send your partner *'immortal flowers.'* You might call them fake flowers, but you can find some very realistic blooms online in a great-looking vase. These flowers will last a very long time.

They will serve as a sort of remembrance anytime your partner looks at them, they will think of you. The flower trick is a sneaky way of remaining top of mind with your partner.

3. A perfect way to cuddle

One thing that most couples miss in their relationship is sexual intimacy. Cuddling is a favorite pastime among people who love each other. There is an easy way to help your partner deal with your absence in a long-distance relationship. Get them a cuddle partner.

I am not talking about another human. Get them a teddy bear or some other stuffed animal. To make sure your partner likes this type of gift, you can subtly have a conversation. This type of gift is a pleasant surprise.

4. Go for a surprise visit

In my opinion, this is the ultimate romantic thing you can do. Paying your partner a surprise visit will not only make their day, but it will serve as a good memory for years to come. If you feel this is something you can do, then you should take the time to plan it well.

Make sure that your partner is not busy during that period. Also, ensure that nothing terrible can spoil your surprise visit. Watch as your partner's eyes light up with happiness.

I must also warn you that a surprise visit can create incredible joy or pain. Your surprise visit may also uncover your partner's failure to honor the commitment made. Use this method at your own risk.

5. Celebrate a special occasion

There are so many special occasions each year. Each celebration gives you a chance to do something nice for your partner. The type of festivals or holidays throughout the year will depend on what part of the world you are from and your religious beliefs.

Since you are in a long-distance relationship, you could order a cake for them. If it is your anniversary, getting them a small gift will work wonders. Always take the festive days as an opportunity to show your partner how much they mean to you.

6. Morning love reminders

In long-distance relationships, you want your partner to have you in front of their eyes. A great way to do this is to send them morning love reminders. These reminders will reveal to your partner that you have them in your thoughts.

This might be very easy to do if you both live in different time zones. Regardless, doing this even once in a while can add positive energy to your relationship.

7. Write letters to each other

Yes, we have email and text messaging now. However, some good old-fashioned love letters can warm the heart. Handwritten letters are often considered very romantic gestures.

Cultivate a habit of writing short letters to your partner, placing them in an envelope, affixing a live stamp, and dropping them in a mailbox. Before long, you will be itching to receive the next letter. Trust me; it is a fantastic feeling.

8. Fall asleep together

Falling asleep together is beautiful and romantic. It shows that you both cannot get enough of each other. The next time both of you are dead tired and cannot have a conversation, don't hesitate to sleep with the video on. Video calls are more effective in making this work.

Grab your phone, jump into bed, prop up your phone using a pillow and start your video call. You both may take turns waking each other up to continue the conversation until you both drift off to sleep. How romantic.

Let's discuss another exciting thing that couples in a long-distance relationship might find appealing.

Romantic Online Games

The thing about romantic games is that it allows both of you to try something new together. Romantic games can add a lot of laughter and fun to a relationship. This is true even if your partner has a competitive streak. To help you on your quest to find good romantic online games, I have composed some of the best that I could find.

1. Truth or Dare

The reason why truth or dare made it onto this list is that it can be anything you want it to be. You can make it clean fun, sexual, or XXX-rated.

You can also make it very romantic by asking questions about your relationship. It gives you a platform to bond about things that you never knew were possible and consolidate on the ones you did.

There are so many apps that allow couples to play this game even across time zones. Do your research and start playing to your heart's content.

2. Board Games

There is not a more familiar game to play online than board games. If you and your partner share a soft spot for board games, then this might be something you should check out.

With board games comes a lot of variety. There are so many games that you can choose from. This includes monopoly, chess, and scramble. If you both played board games before the long-distance started, then this is an excellent thing to do to remind yourself of all the fun you had.

3. The Stripping Game

Playing an online game with each other can be intimate. This is what the stripping game aims to achieve. The game usually requires one person to take off a piece of clothing for every wrong answer they give.

There are numerous ways to play this game. You can play through an app or video calls. The best part of this game is setting and changing the rules. It is bound to be spicy and very entertaining.

4. Charades

You probably played this game in person with friends before. You can also do the same in a long-distance relationship. All you need is Skype or another video app. Watch as one person mimics the word while the other answers.

5. Finding the Next Experience

If you want a connection to your partner's life, then try this game. You get to choose your partner's adventures and vice versa. You can also do this through the use of apps and search engines. Once your partner has gone on your chosen adventures, they send pictures or videos.

Then, you get to go on their chosen experience. It can go on forever, and it is fun. If you have recently moved to a new area, you get to explore your new city and virtually take your partner with you.

6. Picture Puzzle

If you and your partner are looking for a mentally challenging game, the picture puzzle game is the perfect bet. In this game, you send each other pictures of things or places you have been to. The image should make it hard for them to identify what it is.

You can decide what the reward or punishment will be for guessing incorrectly. Making the reward enticing will make the game more interesting.

7. Role Play

There is nothing a bit of role-playing cannot solve. So test out your acting skills with your partner. You can get your role-play career going with the help of a video app.

Skype is a good option. You can be sure that this will be an incredible experience.

Remember that most apps have their own rules and regulations on what is acceptable and not. It is best to do some research on the right app to use that fits your personality.

Tips on Keeping Romance Levels High

Before ending this chapter, I want to give you my best tips on keeping the romance moving smoothly. The longer you both stay apart, the more challenging it will be to keep the romance alive.

If you get lazy about creating romantic experiences, you risk a relationship that will eventually die. Let us go into what you can do to keep the romance spicy.

Find out what your partner wants

The priority is to keep your relationship moving in the right direction. That is not going to happen if your partner is unhappy. As mentioned in the last chapter, every person is different. They also come with their own likes and dislikes.

First, try to find out if your partner is okay with all or any of the ideas you have. It will be quite a bummer to push an idea only to find out that it did not have the desired positive effect on your partner. Let's try to avoid that from happening.

Please don't overdo it

You must be bubbling with so many ideas to try out! The last two chapters have been about how to spice up your relationship. From date ideas to game ideas, I gave you many options to help you stay connected when you both live in distant cities.

While experimenting with these ideas, try not to overdo them. Take it one day at a time. Understand that some days should be left for just talking.

By not overdoing it, you build anticipation for the next idea that you implement. Your partner will also not feel that they are on a rollercoaster.

Although a rollercoaster can be fun at times, some couples face another problem. They may both have kids and no idea about how to handle the situation. Are you in this boat?

If you are, then you need to check out the next chapter.

CHAPTER 12: WHAT IF ONE OR BOTH OF YOU HAVE CHILDREN?

A majority of married couples dream of having children. Miniature versions of your love running around the world can touch even the hardest of hearts. While having children is a mental and emotional thing, it can be stressful.

Managing a long-distance relationship when one or both of you have children adds an extra level of challenge. You might also deal with the stress brought on by your partner's ex-partner. This can be a delicate dance. Is it possible to pull this off? Well, think back to the real-life stories mentioned in chapter two of this program.

Some of these stories were about couples who both had children. These stories prove that others have faced this situation and created successful relationships. You can too. To help you navigate this situation, I want to discuss how to handle children in long-distance relationships.

First, we will look at how to children them if one partner has them. Then, we will look at a situation where both partners have children. Finally, I dive into the nightmare scenario where your kids disapprove of your relationship. What do you do then? Let's get started.

Managing a Long-Distance Relationship When One Partner Has Children

If only one of you have children, here are things you can do to manage your long-distance relationship effectively.

1. Talk about it

You want to talk to your partner about this issue. Managing a child can be a significant factor in how your relationship grows or dies. Talk about issues that might arise.

This is when you need clear and precise communication with your partner. You must understand what you are getting into and manage the situation effectively. Doing this is crucial to the success of your relationship.

2. Get alone together

Raising a child is a full-time job. You must be there for them in many ways. Therefore, finding alone time can be a challenge. The wrinkle is that only one partner has a child. The partner with a child (or children) may struggle to find time to give you, and this will put a strain on that partner and you. It can leave the childless partner lonely in the relationship.

To combat this, schedule time to talk. The partner with a child knows when they have a few minutes each day. Schedule your virtual time together. The childless partner will have to get used to scheduling time with their partner.

As stated earlier, video calls can be the best way to communicate. You can find time on your way home each day or when the kids are out with friends or at school. Talk to your partner and find the best way to fine-tune your schedules to accommodate each other.

3. Consider telling your child

Telling your child *(or children)* about your long-distance relationship depends on your child's age. If your child is old enough to understand relationships, you should probably let them know.

By doing this, you get time to focus on your relationship and not worry about what your child might think because they already know. Sneaking around your house to cover-up your long-distance relationship will make the relationship less fun.

There is always the chance that your child *(or children)* might not like your partner *(we'll talk about this soon)*. However, if your child is not old enough to understand such things, you might want to consider another method. One approach is allowing your child to meet your partner over the phone.

Just a quick *"Say hi to my daughter/son"* breaks the ice. You do not need to give your child details, like telling your child that your partner lives across the Atlantic Ocean.

4. Make time for your child

Give your child *(or children)* as much attention as needed. They should not feel as if you have less time for them now.

Do not cancel time with your child to speak with your partner. Kids can build resentment towards you for months or years and never tell you why. You do not want your child saying to themselves, *"Oh, so this is why mom/dad has so little time for me; it is because of that new person."*

5. Tell your child good things about your partner

This depends on your child's age. Make sure that your child hears many good things about your partner. Tell them how much your partner cares for you and why you love them. If your child is younger, you can tell them the good deeds they have done. Ensuring that your child feels a bit close to your long-distance partner can be game-changing.

Managing the Relationship When Both Partners Have Children

What if both of you have children? While it is pretty similar to the first situation, there are some things you have to bear in mind moving forward.

1. Communication

When you both have children, you and your partner must discuss how you will deal with your kids. At this point, communication is the most important. It might also be a good idea to talk to your children about your relationship.

Helping them understand where you stand will help them to decide how they feel about your partner. It is significant when you discuss these things with your children. It makes them feel like a part of your life. Sneaking around the house to speak to your partner is usually not a good idea.

2. Plan a getaway together

Managing kids might mean bringing everyone together. Perhaps you can plan a getaway trip with your partner and their kids. Make sure that your relationship is stable before doing this.

You want to have a good idea about the temperament your partner's child *(or children)* posses. The first getaway together should be short, not a weekend.

3. Introduce your kids to your partner

Introducing your kids to your partner can be approached in many ways. Both of you can introduce your kids to each other. This also depends on the circumstances of the relationship.

Doing this depends on the level of the relationship. Another thing you have to consider is the ages of the kids. If the kids are in the same age bracket, introducing them might work nicely, especially if they have the same interests: like in sports, the arts, technology, etc.

4. Never abandon spending time alone together

Amid all the chaos that children can bring, never forget your relationship. A long-distance relationship can be a challenge without kids. Ensure that you find time to spend with your partner every day *(or at least every other day)*.

The quality of time that you spend with your partner makes the most significant impact. Throw some personal visits in the mix, and your relationship will remain fresh. However, your kids might just not like your partner or vice-versa.

How on earth do you handle that situation? Your goal should not be to fix the problem. You cannot force people to like each other if the energy between them does not mix organically. The best thing to do is manage the situation to reduce the chances of it hurting your relationship.

What to Do if Your Child *(or Children)* Do Not Like Your Long-Distance Partner

This can happen, and you must prepare for it mentally. I can give you strategies to manage this unfortunate situation, but you cannot force people to like anyone. If your kids find it hard liking your partner, that will hurt. Here are some things you can do to manage this issue.

1. Try to understand the root cause

Your children are a big part of your lives. This means that how they feel matters to you. You need to know why your child does not care for your partner. This is important for various reasons.

Sometimes, kids might not like your new partner because they feel that this person will take you away. It might be that they think the new partner is there to replace their parent, making it impossible for you to reconcile and be a family again.

It could also be a painful reminder that you are no longer with their parent. Once you know the root cause of the dislike, you can know the next step to take.

2. Are you bothered by the action?

This is mainly related to the age of your child. If you have much smaller kids, then the initial hate might pass with time. You have to ask yourself if you feel bothered by it so much that you want to resolve the matter. If not, then you should probably wait for it to pass.

3.   Discuss the issue with your child

If you have found the root cause of the dislike, your next step is to discuss this matter with your child. It might be a good time to articulate to your child how their displeasure makes you feel.

Your feelings matter as well. If your child knows that their dislike for your partner hurts you, they may put aside their negative emotions. If you think that the relationship will lead to marriage, this is an excellent time to tell your child.

During this conversation, help your child understand why you love your partner. Point out your partner's best qualities and how much they make you happy. During this conversation, ensure that your child's dislike is not a way to control your attention. If so, you should reassure your child that you are not going anywhere.

4.   Make sure that your child is involved

Perhaps your child does not seem comfortable with your partner because they do not know them. Look for small opportunities for them to meet and talk. Long-distance relationships might not have enough opportunities for this to happen. However, video calls and occasional visits might be the best way to start.

Maybe your partner has expertise in a passion your child needs advice about. Asking your partner to talk to your child for 5-minutes can do wonders. Helping your child establish a positive relationship with your partner might slowly turn you into a third wheel.

Managing a long-distance relationship with kids can be a challenging task. The tips mentioned will help you make progress. Talking about recommendations, here are some tips that I recommend if you want your kids to respond well to your relationship.

Tips on Managing Kids in a Long-Distance Relationship

1. You have to be patient

Just like other parts of your children's lives, this is the time to be patient. You must show a lot of restraint. This is not the time to command your kids to give your partner a chance.

It is also not the time to have a heated conversation about the issue. Your child is human, and you cannot force people to like each other for your benefit.

2. It may not be a stroll in the park

While this process might seem smooth and doable

now, it is different in reality. Your kids will test your patience. Your partner will get worried if your kids do not like them.

Things may get tense. Prepare yourself mentally for all these eventualities, and do not freak-out. You have a guide in your hands to refer to.

3. Don't get sucked into the trap

While some of your child's concerns about your partner will be genuine and should be considered, others will not. Children usually seek the attention of their parents. Accommodating another person competing for that attention will be very unwelcome.

Make sure that you do not cave to this behavior. This can put unnecessary strain on your relationship. While others might tell you to break up with your partner if your child disapproves, this is not always a good move. You do not want your child to have total control over who you date.

So there you have it. This could be the most significant issue you must handle in a long-distance relationship. However, if your child immediately likes your partner, it can become quite a blessing. It can even become the bond that holds both of you together.

If they do not like your partner, following the tips mentioned will help. Perhaps, you both might soon transition into living in the same city. This brings its own challenges and why it is a befitting discussion for the next chapter.

See you in the next chapter!

CHAPTER 13: TRANSITIONING TO LIVING IN THE SAME CITY TOGETHER

After following the tips in this program and staying committed to your relationship, your dreams finally come true. You and your partner will finally start living in the same city! You feel excited, happy and cannot help but dance. However, you also feel a little bit of fear.

Both of you are not used to living in the same city. It gets more complicated if you both want to live together in the same house. Do you know each other well enough not to drive each other crazy?

Will living together turn a great relationship into a nightmare? Maybe you both should not live in the same house but live separately in the same city for a while. These are questions that every couple has to ask themselves.

It might seem like the heavy lifting is done when

long-distance couples move into the same city. However, this issue can quickly descend into chaos and make the relationship end abruptly.

This chapter details how to make your relationship work while transitioning to the same city. I explain why you need to be clear and straightforward about your *'deal-breakers'* if you have chosen to live together. After you conclude this chapter, you will be well-equipped to deal with the challenges that lie ahead.

Deciding Whether to Live Together or Separately

When the time comes for you to live in the same city, you might feel excited. However, you face a difficult decision. Should you both live together immediately or live separately for a few months? I would recommend that you and your partner live apart for some time before moving into the same place. Here are a few reasons why.

1. It avoids being overwhelmed

While you and your partner have probably spoken to each other frequently during your long-distance relationship, your interaction under the same roof will be very different. People like their own space and you are no different. Your partner might have never been with you for more than a few days.

To ensure that neither of you feel overwhelmed by

the new setup, it might be wise to gradually spend more time with each other. In no time, you'll be living under the same roof.

2. It allows for time to learn each other's habits

When you live separately in the same city, you can gradually spend more hours together and learn each other's habits. You can build exposure to each other weekly. First, two days a week. The next week, three days a week, and then add a day each week until you get to 5 to 7 days a week if you want maximum exposure to each other.

3. It gives time to settle in

While transitioning your relationship to the same city is exciting, remember that it is still a new move for both of you. One or both of you will have to explore the city, maybe build a new social circle, and find a job.

It might be best to live apart during this process for a while. One or both of you might want to settle in without feeling crowded.

How to Ease Your Way into Living Together

The best way to ease into living together is to alternate 3 to 4 consecutive days of living together over a weekend. Starting on a Friday, for 3 to 4 days, you stay at your partner's place. The next Friday, for 3 to 4 days, your partner stays at your home. In the middle of the week, you both stay separately to breathe. This process allows both of you to get a good idea of how living together might be.

This process gives both of you the chance to experience any annoying habits your partner views as *'normal.'*

You can adjust slowly to accepting the habit, and they can do the same about your annoying habits. You should have a heart-to-heart talk if your partner engages in habits you cannot accept.

Finances might prevent you from living separately, especially if one partner does not have a job in the new city. It would be best for that partner first to get a new job before you both move to the same city.

If the plan is to live in an expensive city, your partner getting a new job might not support living on their own. Lack of financial power might reduce your options, and you must move in together from the start. With that said, let's talk about how to live together.

How to Handle Living Together

What if you decide to live together immediately? In general, I feel that people should watch a few YouTube videos about living together before making the leap. Here are tips that will make the transition smooth.

1. Give each other space

You probably want to consume every minute with your partner. However, you must give each other space. Usually, one partner needs more space than the other.

You might not realize which one of you requires the most space because long-distance dating provided plenty of space by default. You want to feel this out and not be shocked if your partner gets a bit distant in the home.

It means that they require more space than you. Just give them space and do not assume that something is wrong.

2. Have your own social circle

Living together can be exciting. However, make sure you retain your friends in that city and help your partner establish their own friends. Encourage them to volunteer and meet new people. You should have your own support system that is separate from your partner's.

Even with great intentions, relationships can still fall apart. While you certainly are not praying for that to happen, you should give yourself something to fall back to.

Moving in with each other certainly has its own challenges. For that reason, one important thing you need to do is to set realistic expectations and deal breakers.

3. Have a bit of patience

The chances are that it will be a bit awkward adjusting to living with someone. Have patience because your partner is probably going through the same challenge. With some excellent communication, you will figure it out quickly. Your love for your partner should see you through this period.

Settling Realistic Expectations and Deal Breakers

One thing that most couples complain about when they move in together is the experience in general. It is just not what they had expected. For that reason, it is better to set realistic expectations of how things will go.

It is best to have a long conversation with your partner. Living together or just being in the same city can have its own cons. So make sure that you understand what you can expect from your partner. Most people fail to do this and are shocked when their relationship takes a nose dive into chaos. Both of you must be completely honest here.

It's important to consider what many refer to as deal-breakers. Deal breakers are things that you absolutely cannot tolerate in a relationship. Before you move in together, you want to open up and discuss these things with your partner.

Most people assume that because their partner has seen their annoying habits in the past, that everything will be fine. This cannot be further from the truth.

Being in a long-distance relationship and living together are two very different things. What your partner might have tolerated when you visited each other over a weekend will be different once in the same house 24-hours a day.

This is not the time to feel offended or attack your partner. Try to make the relationship work by making reasonable compromises.

Deal-breakers might mean that living together will not be possible. It might be wise to live apart for some time. During this time, you can reassess the relationship to see if it is something you can deal with. Apart from deal-breakers, there is another crucial thing to consider during this transition period.

Why Keeping Your Own Space Can Preserve Your Sanity and Relationship

Keeping your own space may seem ridiculous when you have been in a long-distance relationship for more than a year. However, it is necessary. You both need space at times. To help persuade you that this is the right course of action, I have documented some of the best reasons why this is necessary. So let's dive in!

1. Self-Development

When you and your partner move to the same city, it

is understandably an exciting time for both of you. You will spend the next couple of weeks by each other's side. This excitement can lead to a severe problem; you may forget to take care of yourself.

Taking care of yourself here means self-development. Self-development will help you become more confident with yourself. It will also allow you to be independent and contribute meaningfully to the relationship. So strive for that first if you want your relationship to last.

2. It strengthens the bond

You have been in a long-distance relationship for some while. But the joy of having your partner next to you will slowly fade to normalcy. You can avoid this fade in excitement by giving each other space.

Giving each other space allows your partner to miss you a bit. When you connect, it is more intense. This does not mean to ignore your partner when they try to connect with you. It does not mean you have to be aloof. It merely means that you have your own thing going on for you.

3. It gives you time for family and friends

While your partner makes up a good portion of your life, they are not your complete package. You still have family and friends. Some of these people were probably in your life before your partner! By giving yourself space, you can interact and create meaningful relationships with other people.

There are times when your loved ones may struggle or go through difficult times—being there to help them can make all the world's difference.

4. It can help you build your relationship

Giving each other space can give you both time to grow the relationship. You will be able to take a step back and see areas that can be improved. For a relationship to last, this is important. Not taking a step back can sometimes lead to problems moving forward.

Having space in a relationship is essential for constant growth and happiness. To end this chapter, I will leave you with my recommended tips on keeping your relationship healthy after your same city transition is completed.

Tips to Keep Your Relationship Healthy After the Transition Process

You might feel as if your mission is complete. You finally live in the same city with your partner after months or even years of dating each other long distance.

The next phase of your relationship is about to begin and requires a different set of success skills.

Keep doing the same things

The work put into keeping the relationship alive in a long-distance relationship is tasking. It might be tempting to get lazy and put less energy into your relationship now that you both live in the same city. While you no longer need to have many video calls and online dates, you must keep things exciting.

You should take time to go on dates with your partner. Make sure you go on adventures and find new things to do together to keep things moving in the right direction.

Don't lose yourself

A romantic relationship means that you and your partner share certain traits. However, make sure that you do not lose yourself in the process. Remember your values and stand up for yourself. In the worst-case scenario, you will be able to get back on your feet if there is a breakup.

Love your partner

I touched on this before, but I want to mention it again. It is easy to get lazy once your partner lives in the same city. Striving to keep the burning fire of excitement going because your partner is excited about you today does not guarantee that their feelings will remain forever. Make sure that your partner knows how much you value and appreciate them.

Prove that you value and appreciate them by keeping things exciting. If your partner is moving into your city, you are probably their backbone and only support system. Transitioning to living in the same city with your partner can bring many challenges.

It can be fascinating and a turning point for better or worse in your relationship. Most couples who get to this stage have seen their relationship blossom into marriage or something close to it.

However, sometimes, your long-distance relationship might never reach the point where you move in together. Sometimes it might end due to the long-distance. The next chapter will help you to handle that sad eventuality if it does occur.

See you in the next chapter!

CHAPTER 14: ENDING THE RELATIONSHIP BECAUSE OF DISTANCE

Sometimes things do not go as planned. That is okay. The world is full of opportunities and endless potential. However, it can hurt if what goes wrong is your long-distance relationship. This is especially true after investing so much time, effort, and money.

I know how that feels. While breaking up is the hardest part of ending a relationship, there are other difficult moments. For example, how do you know when to end the relationship? Should you give your long-distance relationship more time? It gets even worse.

What if someone breaks up with you unexpectedly? How do you cope with the hurt and confusion that might follow? This chapter addresses these questions. Knowing when to end a relationship can help you save precious time and resources.

To begin, let's look at signs that the end of your relationship is looming.

Signs That You Might Need To End Your Long-Distance Relationship

1. Absence of trust

I mentioned the need for trust and faith in earlier chapters. I discussed how an absence of trust could lead to other problems. It is not surprising that loss of trust is one of the most significant signs that there is a problem with your relationship.

If you cannot trust your partner in a long-distance relationship, nothing will work. Doubts about infidelity quickly infect your mind. You no longer want to give your partner the benefit of the doubt because you have seen too many signs that you cannot trust them.

When one or both partners no longer trust, it leads to a relationship that has little value. It might be time to call the relationship quits.

2. You do not have the same future plans

In long-distance relationships, one of the very prevalent things is planning for the future. You both plan to transition the long-distance into a same-city relationship. One sign that the relationship might have to end is when your plans do not match.

If you both will not be in the same city in the next one to five years, a long-distance relationship might not work. Discuss transitioning to the same city as soon as you can. Make sure you get enough assurance that the distance gap will close. Look for actions that prove that things are moving in the right direction.

3. Communication problems

Lack of communication can mean the end is near. Couples can have many problems because of poor communication or a lack of it over time. This really can end a relationship.

If you and your partner cannot communicate or understand each other, it might be time to end the relationship. Of course, this should not be done immediately. You should take steps to determine if you can address this problem. If your efforts repeatedly fail, then maybe it is time to move on.

4. You are the only one who puts in the effort

A long-distance relationship is a lot of work. It gets more complicated if one partner refuses to put in the desired effort. Some effort might be easy, but one partner shows a lack of interest.

For example, just taking the time to text first can be considered an effort. You can also send gifts from time to time. If your partner does not do the easy stuff and always seems busy, you should consider breaking up.

5. Sexual spark is gone

We had a whole chapter dedicated to integrating

intimacy into your long-distance relationship. It included sexting, video calls, and other spicy adventures. However, if your partner does not seem interested in igniting your sexual life, this can be hard to deal with.

Your partner might have some boundaries regarding this issue. This should be considered before deciding. If this is one of your deal-breakers, it could be a sign that things will not work out. Sexual incompatibility is a valid reason to terminate a relationship. If your partner can not *'ring your bells,'* it is time to move on.

6. Lack of physical presence

Despite being in a long-distance relationship, you still need to see each other once in a while. In long-distance relationships, you must plan your time and finances to make this happen. If your partner is not ready to make plans that match your schedule, something might be wrong.

Of course, situations differ. Sometimes, your partner might be available on a weekend that does not work for you. They might have taken the initiative on several occasions. If both of you cannot create availability that matches and months go by without visiting each other, you need to re-think the relationship.

If you are not feeling satisfied in a long-distance relationship, you should consider breaking up. If you have already made up your mind about breaking up, you should discuss this with your partner.

Finding The Right Way To Break Up

Breaking away from a long-distance relationship is different from a same-city relationship. You must decide if you will wait to see the person or do it over the phone. In my opinion, it is best to break up over a video chat. It makes no sense to spend money to visit someone to break up with them because now there is a financial loss that did not have to take place.

It is not advisable to break up over text messages. Text messages are often viewed as impersonal. The person you are breaking up with deserves some form of closure to help them understand what went wrong. If you are going to break up over the phone *(or video)*, here are some tips that will help you through this tough time.

Tell them you need to talk

The first step is to tell your partner that you need to talk. It might be advisable to schedule a time when none of you will be interrupted. If both of you already have a scheduled call, this might be the best time to break the news.

Some people come to expect a breakup when it starts with specific words. Words like *"we have to talk"* are now straightforward ways to communicate impending doom in a relationship. This will allow them to prepare their minds for what is to come.

Handling the conversation

Once you have them on the call, slowly break the bad news. Make sure they understand the reasons why this is happening. Do not use this moment as an opportunity to attack them for what has happened in the relationship.

You want to be as firm as possible. If this is something you want to do, make sure that you do not change your mind. This is no time to be wishy-washy.

Give them a chance for closure

While the relationship is at its end, it is always good for people to have closure. Allow them to express themselves and how they feel about the matter. Once everything that should be said has been discussed, do not waste time before hanging up. It shows that you are serious about your intentions.

Get rid of their items

The chances are that you have a couple of your partner's things with you. Perhaps this happened when they came over for visits. Regardless, this is the time for you to pack up their items and send them back to them or throw them out.

To deal with a breakup, you must focus on yourself first. This becomes more important if the roles are reversed. How do you cope and heal if your long-distance partner breaks up with you?

How To Heal If Your Partner Breaks Up With You

First, you should know that you will be alright eventually. Time heals a lot of deep wounds. However, to fast-track the process, here are some tips to help.

1.   Do not deny your emotions

The fastest way to be stuck mourning a relationship is to deny the feeling that comes with a breakup. Admit that you feel bad. Cry if you must. This allows you to get emotional stress out of the way. It also allows you to look to the future without any form of longing for the past. It helps you to know that the breakup was real.

2.   Take time to focus on yourself

After a breakup, focus on yourself. Do not waste energy planning your revenge. Take care of your body and ensure that you do not turn to harmful coping mechanisms; drugs, alcohol, random sex. This will only compound the issue for you. As you focus on yourself, you will boost your confidence levels. That can be helpful.

3.   Go out with friends

Before your ex-partner came into your life, you had a life. Now that your partner is gone, your life does not have to stop. Make sure you keep your support system in the loop about how you are coping. Also, take time to go and have fun. It might be difficult, but it is an opportunity to forget about the breakup for one night.

4.   Count your blessings

You are probably at a stage where all you feel is hurt and disappointment. You might be angry that you invested so much time and resources. However, you must take time out to count your blessings. First, you are alive and well. You also probably have a job and a life to live. You might also have kids and friends who love you.

By counting your blessing, you will realize that things are never as bad as they seem.

5.   Be a volunteer

One thing that helps people cope with breakups is volunteering. You feel joy when you give back to communities. Volunteer your time with an organization or charity. This will give you time away from your thoughts and help you focus on others for a while. You might find someone new, if just for a friendship.

6.   Stay away from your ex-partner

This is easy to do in a long-distance relationship because they are miles away. However, your partner is probably active on some social media platforms. You might have special apps where you strengthened your bonds together. Delete these apps and your ex-partner's contact details. Avoid your partner's social media accounts to see what they are up to. You can mute them or even block them. All that matters right now is your mental health. Please do what you must to preserve it.

To end this chapter, I want to give you additional tips on dealing with the entire process of breaking up.

Tips On Dealing With Breakups in a Long-Distance Relationship

1.   There are still others out there

If you thought your partner was your soul mate or was simply perfect, a breakup might have dampened your spirit. The truth is that there are still people out there. You will find someone new who adores you. Keep your eyes and heart open.

2.   Your mental health comes first

When dealing with a breakup, you must put yourself first. Take as much time as you want to heal. Do not feel inclined to rush into a new relationship. It is simply not worth it.

3.   Make sure a breakup is really what you want

Finally, do not be in a hurry to break up. Make sure you look at the pros and cons. Doing so ensures that you will not make a regrettable decision. It will also ensure that you do not hurt your partner unnecessarily.

Breaking up after a long-distance relationship is never

easy. Sometimes, it just has to happen. Dealing with it might be tricky. However, it will lead to growth and self-improvement. It might even lead to a new partner who possesses superior qualities to your previous partner. This happens more often than you realize.

In the end, I'm sure that you will be just fine. Let's wrap up this long-distance blueprint in the last chapter.

See you in the next chapter!

CONCLUSION

All good things come to an end. We have reached the end of this program, and it has been an incredible adventure. This resource should have been a learning process if you are in a long-distance relationship.

Here is the thing; It is always tricky when faced with a long-distance problem. You might not feel like you are going to make it. Perhaps your last long-distance relationship did not go so well. You might also be facing resistance from loved ones. Perhaps they are concerned about your relationship's effect on your finances.

You might also have to plan a lot of trips across great distances. This might take a lot of time and effort on your part. It can get more challenging when dealing with children in a long-distance relationship. Add to that; how do you even keep the relationship's spark going strong?

This is precisely what this program has been about. It is here to tell you that it is possible to have a long-distance relationship despite these challenges. It raises you from the depth of worry and gives you much-needed hope moving forward. To round out this program, let's look at some of the essential points you should take with you.

Important Points That Will Keep Your Long-Distance Relationship Strong

1. It's all about your mindset

Sometimes, a long-distance relationship's success and failure will come down to your mindset. If you do not feel your relationship will succeed initially, you have already failed.

Developing the right mindset for a long-distance relationship might not be easy. However, taking steps such as educating yourself about long-distance relationships is vital. By executing the methods in this program, you have taken the first step towards achieving that.

Now you have to implement the things you have learned in your relationship.

2. Communication is important

Communication with your partner has been a recurring theme throughout this program. That is because it is essential. Learn how to communicate with your partner. Technology has made this easy. Download the right apps. Have regular video calls. Make the most of the moment.

While speaking to them, make sure that you listen to what they have to say. Consider their opinions seriously. That provides the right platform for the relationship to progress. It also helps when you are having doubts about your partner's fidelity.

3. Be kind and firm to family and loved ones

Everyone might not like your long-distance relationship, and that is okay. However, this might include your parents and even your friends. When this happens, you must display restraint and kindness when dealing with them.

Try to understand why they feel the relationship is bad for you. Do this while remaining firm. It might also be helpful to be objective. Sometimes, your friends and family might raise genuine points that need to be considered.

4. Learn how to deal with problems and arguments

If there is one thing present in a relationship, it is arguments and disagreement. The need to argue and disagree healthily has significantly been discussed in this program. Once again, it all boils down to how you communicate with your partner. Learning to deal with problems and arguments will significantly reduce the growth of resentment and anger.

5. Issues must be resolved

You will have particular issues you must resolve. For example, both of you must sit down and talk about your relationship's financial part. The question of who pays for what at every given time is better discussed before the time is necessary.

This program has also addressed when it might be time to leave a relationship. You should leave a relationship when there are signs of abuse or when your future plans do not align.

How This Program Has Helped You Along Your Journey

When you started this program, I talked about the trouble zones in a relationship. Throughout the remaining chapters, trouble zones were not mentioned! Refer back to this section often throughout your relationship.

You learned how to keep your sexual intimacy growing strong in a long-distance relationship. Financial disparities and travel schedules have also been discussed at great lengths. This program has also provided you with concrete tips to help you deal with insecurity in a relationship. Applying them will prove to be the best thing you can do.

I have given you romantic ideas that can keep things exciting and fun. Arguments will always come up. This program has outlined some of the best ways to settle disputes without ruining your relationship. I also emphasized the need to develop communication strategies. These strategies will keep the communication doors open and help your relationship head in the right direction.

There are so many techniques and things you have to learn in a long-distance relationship. Sometimes, you learn these things while in the relationship itself. For the most part, this program can guide you to having the most successful long-distance relationship possible.

What You Absolutely Must Know About Long-Distance Relationships

Before wrapping up this incredible journey, here is the one thing I would love you to know and understand. **Every relationship is unique.** Therefore, what works for your friend or your family member might not work for you and your partner.

Also, not every point in this program will be good for your relationship. Every relationship has its own language. Add to this circumstantial situation, and you will realize that a relationship can never be put in a box.

Have fun with your partner. Communicate with them always. Trust and love them. Give them the benefit of the doubt. All these things should be done in a normal relationship. However, being in a long-distance relationship makes it more critical.

In the end, you will be happy and satisfied with your long-distance relationship. That is my number one desire for you and your partner.

If you enjoyed this program, please make sure you grab your free gift on the next page.

Grab Your FREE Gift on the Next Page

YOUR FREE GIFT

Long Distance Love Tips Sheet

Sometimes you need a quick tip for a situation. This tips sheet points you to the best resources to help you fast!
(Get Yours Now...It's FREE)

Request FREE Tips Sheet Today. Go to:
https://LoveBlueprints.com/love-tips-sheet/

Reference List

Smith, E. W. (2019b, September 9). *How To Tell It's Time To End Your Long-Distance Relationship.* Refinery29. https://www.refinery29.com/en-us/when-to-end-long-distance-relationship-over

H. (2016, January 13). *4 Tips for Transitioning From a Long-Distance Relationship to Living in the Same Place.* Glamour. https://www.glamour.com/story/4-tips-for-transitioning-from

A. (2020, August 22). *Why Having Space in a Relationship Is Important.* Make Me Better. https://www.makemebetter.net/why-having-space-in-a-relationship-is-important/

Watson, G. (2019, October 16). *The Ugly Truth about Long-Distance Relationships.* The Odyssey Online. https://www.theodysseyonline.com/ugly-truth-about-long-distance-relations

Smith, E. W. (2019, September 5). *9 Real Statistics About Long-Distance Relationships.* Refinery29.

https://www.refinery29.com/en-us/long-distance-relationship-statistics

Petersen, R. (2020, November 8). *5 Well-Researched Long-Distance Relationship Statistics (2020 Update)*. Dating at a Distance. https://datingatadistance.com/long-distance-relationship-statistics/

Editorial Team. (2020, June 2). *Long-distance Relationship Statistics 2020 – Backed by Research*. Friendship Lamps. https://www.friendlamps.com/blog/long-distance-relationship-statistics-research/#:%7E:text=A%20large%20portion%20of%20that,in%20a%20long%2Ddistance%20relationship

Gartner, M. (2020, November 13). *"My Parents Don't Approve of My LDR."* Long Distance Relationships Blog. https://longdistancerelationships.blog/my-parents-dont-approve-of-my-long-distance-relationship/

Roiz, J. (2019, January 31). *10 Things My Friends Will Never Understand About My Long-Distance Relationship*. VIX. https://www.vix.com/en/relationships/529448/10-things-my-friends-will-never-understand-about-my-long-distance-relationship

Shatto, R. (2019, June 6). *If Your Friends Don't Support Your Relationship, Here's What Experts Suggest*. Elite Daily. https://www.elitedaily.com/p/if-your-friends-dont-support-your-relationship-heres-what-experts-suggest-17983933

Bennett, B., & Steber, C. (2020, March 24). *17 Apps That Will Make Long-Distance Couples Feel Like They're Closer Together*. Bustle. https://www.bustle.com/p/17-apps-that-will-make-long-distance-couples-feel-like-theyre-closer-together-2985152

HuffPost is now a part of Verizon Media. (2019). Verizon Media. https://www.huffpost.com/entry/sex-tips-long-distance-

relationship_l_5cacfc1ce4b0e833aa323de9?gucc
ounter=1

How Much is your relationship costing you? (2019, March 21).
Money Under 30.
https://www.moneyunder30.com/the-financial-
realities-of-a-long-distance-romance

McKay, L. (2018, March 28). *13 Tips for Dealing With
Different Time Zones In A Long Distance
Relationship.* Make Your Long Distance
Relationship Easy & Fun | Modern Love Long
Distance.
https://www.modernlovelongdistance.com/diff
erent-time-zones-long-distance-relationship/

Strong, R. (2020, March 2). *How To Trust Your Long-
Distance Partner If You're Worried About Cheating.*
Elite Daily. https://www.elitedaily.com/p/how-
to-trust-your-long-distance-partner-if-youre-
worried-about-cheating-22513407

Leguizamon, M. (2017, April 7). *Here's Why Being Clingy
Is the Worst Relationship Mistake.* Elite Daily.

https://www.elitedaily.com/dating/being-clingy-worst-relationshp-mistake/1851397#:%7E:text=Being%20clingy%20makes%20you%20more,already%20an%20extremely%20clingy%20person.

Villalon, C. (2021, January 8). *How to Resolve Trust Issues in a Long Distance Relationship*. Inspiring Tips. https://inspiringtips.com/resolve-trust-issues-long-distance-relationship/

7 Tips for Handling Conflict in Your Relationship. (2020, November 13). One Love Foundation. https://www.joinonelove.org/learn/handling_conflict/

8 Things Successful Couples do Differently during an Argument. (n.d.). Verizon Media. https://www.huffpost.com/entry/8-things-successful-couples-do-differently-during-arguments_n_569fd4f0e4b0875553c2a5e0?guccounter=1

Wendy, D. (2018, October 10). *8 Tips For Transitioning out of a Long Distance Relationship*. Dear Wendy. https://dearwendy.com/8-tips-for-transitioning-from-a-long-distance-relationship-to-living-nearby/

wikiHow. (2020, December 25). *How to Get Over a Break Up*. https://www.wikihow.com/Get-Over-a-Break-Up

Ohlin, B. (2020, November 7). *7 Ways to Improve Communication in Relationships*. PositivePsychology.Com. https://positivepsychology.com/communication-in-relationships/

Department of Health & Human Services. (2014, August 31). *Relationships and communication*. Better Health Channel. https://www.betterhealth.vic.gov.au/health/healthyliving/relationships-and-communication

Howard, L. (2019, January 23). *Here's How Experts Define Healthy Communication In A Relationship*. Bustle.

https://www.bustle.com/p/heres-how-experts-define-healthy-communication-in-a-relationship-15830872

sarahccbence@gmail.com. (2021, February 9). *27 Long Distance Date Ideas That Will Keep You Going When You're Apart*. Endless Distances. https://www.endlessdistances.com/27-long-distance-date-ideas/

Prokopets, E. (2018, January 17). *15 Cool And Practical Apps For Couples*. Lifehack. https://www.lifehack.org/articles/technology/15-cool-and-practical-apps-for-couples.html

G. (2020b, April 21). *20 Romantic Gifts For Couples In Long Distance Relationships*. Make Your Long Distance Relationship Easy & Fun | Modern Love Long Distance. https://www.modernlovelongdistance.com/romantic-gifts-couples-long-distance/

TodayWeDate.com. (2020, March 27). *20 Romantic Long Distance Relationship Activities To Keep Love Alive.*

Today We Date.
https://todaywedate.com/long-distance-date-ideas/

357

L. (2017, April 21). *How To Make Long Distance Relationship Work If You Have Kids?* Overcoming The Distance.
https://overcomingthedistance.com/advice/ldr-with-kids/

www.ingramcontent.com/pod-product-compliance
Lightning Source LLC
Chambersburg PA
CBHW020905060726
47591CB00004B/1101